Praise for *The Long-Distance Leader*

"Kevin Eikenberry and Wayne Turmel have teamed up to produce the single best guide on remote leadership on the market today. Based on research with real-life practicing managers, *The Long-Distance Leader* offers nineteen rules that guide remote leaders through the most pressing challenges they face—everything from the best use of technology, to effective long-distance coaching, to achieving goals, to building trust at a distance. And even if you aren't a long-distance leader, at least not yet, you will definitely want to have this book handy. As the authors rightfully acknowledge and our research supports, you have to 'think leadership first, location second.' The engaging stories, the practical wisdom, and the reflection and action questions will help you improve your leadership wherever you and your followers are."

—**Jim Kouzes, coauthor of the bestselling *The Leadership Challenge* and Dean's Executive Fellow of Leadership, Leavey School of Business, Santa Clara University**

"Finally, a superb leadership book with a purpose: dealing with the challenges of long-distance leadership. A must-read for leaders of all organizations dealing with the increasing demand for and challenge of long-distance leadership. As global economies force more and more organizations to deal with this leadership challenge, this book provides a well-thought-out and practical guide you will want all your leaders to inculcate."

—**Major General David Ralston (US Army, Retired)**

"When I discuss what a leader is with midlevel managers, this book will be on the reference list for them. They can assess themselves on the leadership skills ladder, establish goals, and work directly with their managers and mentors. I particularly like the 'check-in' section . . . I find my development participants increase their impact and performance with the knowledge they have a voice and are thought about, even though their leaders might physically see them only once a year . . . A practical approach to the journey of success as a remote leader . . . We should all consider what skill we are going to focus on today."

—**Alicia Davis, Director, Global Finance Learning and Development, Dell Inc.**

"Leaders who are determined to make an impact in the fiercely complex world of the 21st century will benefit greatly from the insights and principles in the *The Long-Distance Leader*."

—**Doug Conant, founder and CEO, ConantLeadership; Chairman, Kellogg Executive Leadership Institute, Northwestern University; former Chairman, Avon Products; and former CEO, Campbell Soup Company**

"Leadership isn't easy. Working remotely adds a new dynamic. The practical tips in this book give readers the edge they need to be successful leading remote teams. Many teams struggle with communication; add the component that you have remote employees and it gets more difficult. The tools in this book give you what you need to be a better leader, as well as the competitive advantage to get the most out of your remote teams."
—Marcie Van Note, MBA Director, Mount Mercy University

"Wayne and Kevin's book offers the reader a solid foundation in leadership in any circumstance and layers it with virtual leadership or leadership at a distance. It is full of nuance and nudges that will help you navigate through the labyrinths of leading at a distance. I especially appreciated the snippets where Wayne and Kevin reveal their ways of working together; this added a very real and personal touch. I encourage you to purchase the book, study the rules, reflect on their questions, put the book into practice, and become a leader who can 'go the distance.'"
—David Zinger, founder and host of the Employee Engagement Network

"Great book. Spot-on timewise. Moving from 'managing' people to 'leading' people has never been more relevant when overnight everything we do as a business could change. A manager manages people; a leader employs great people and trusts them to achieve amazing results."
—Ann Andrews, CSP, author of *Lessons in Leadership*

The Long-Distance Leader
Rules for Remarkable Remote Leadership

Kevin Eikenberry and Wayne Turmel

Berrett–Koehler Publishers, Inc.
a BK Business book

Berrett-Koehler Publishers, Inc.
1333 Broadway, Suite 1000
Oakland, CA 94612-1921
Tel: (510) 817-2277
Fax: (510) 817-2278
www.bkconnection.com

ORDERING INFORMATION
Quantity sales. Special discounts are available on quantity purchases by corporations, associations, and others. For details, contact the "Special Sales Department" at the Berrett-Koehler address above.
Individual sales. Berrett-Koehler publications are available through most bookstores. They can also be ordered directly from Berrett-Koehler: Tel: (800) 929-2929; Fax: (802) 864-7626; www.bkconnection.com.
Orders for college textbook/course adoption use. Please contact Berrett-Koehler: Tel: (800) 929-2929; Fax: (802) 864-7626.
Distributed to the U.S. trade and internationally by Penguin Random House Publisher Services.
Berrett-Koehler and the BK logo are registered trademarks of Berrett-Koehler Publishers, Inc.

Printed in the United States of America

Berrett-Koehler books are printed on long-lasting acid-free paper. When it is available, we choose paper that has been manufactured by environmentally responsible processes. These may include using trees grown in sustainable forests, incorporating recycled paper, minimizing chlorine in bleaching, or recycling the energy produced at the paper mill.

Library of Congress Cataloging-in-Publication Data
Names: Eikenberry, Kevin, 1962- author. | Turmel, Wayne, author.
Title: The long-distance leader : rules for remarkable remote leadership / Kevin Eikenberry and Wayne Turmel.
Description: First edition. | Oakland, California : Berrett-Koehler Publishers, [2018] | Includes bibliographical references.
Identifiers: LCCN 2018003596 | ISBN 9781523094615 (pbk.)
Subjects: LCSH: Leadership.
Classification: LCC HD57.7 .E384 2018 | DDC 658.4/092--dc23
LC record available at https://lccn.loc.gov/2018003596

First Edition
23 22 21 20 19   10 9 8 7 6 5 4 3

Interior design and production: Dovetail Publishing Services
Cover design and production: Adrian Morgan
Cover photo: SkillUp/Shutterstock.com

This book is dedicated to our teammates at The Kevin Eikenberry Group and Remote Leadership Institute for being our inspiration, our support, and occasionally our lab rats. You are all truly remarkable.

Contents

Rules for Remarkable Remote Leadership

Rule 1   Think about leadership first, location second.

Rule 2   Accept the fact that leading remotely requires you to lead differently.

Rule 3   Know that working remotely changes the interpersonal dynamics, even if you don't want it to.

Rule 4   Use technology as a tool, not as a barrier or an excuse.

Rule 5   Leading requires a focus on outcomes, others, and ourselves.·

Rule 6   Leading successfully requires achieving goals of many types.

Rule 7   Focus on achieving goals, not just setting them.

Rule 8   Coach your team effectively regardless of where they work.

Rule 9   Communicate in the ways that work best for others rather than based on your personal preferences. ← *Disagree* (handwritten)

Rule 10   Leading successfully requires understanding what people are · thinking, not just what they are doing.

Rule 11   Building trust at a distance doesn't happen by accident.

Rule 12   Identify the leadership results you need, then select the communication tool to achieve them.

Rule 13   Maximize a tool's capabilities or you'll minimize your effectiveness.

Rule 14   Seek feedback to best serve outcomes, others, and ourselves.

Rule 15   Examine your beliefs and self-talk—they define how you lead.

Rule 16 (circled)   Accept that you can't do it all—you shouldn't try anyway.

Rule 17   Balance your priorities to be a Remarkable Long-Distance Leader.

Rule 18   Ensure your leadership development prepares Long-Distance Leaders.

Rule 19   When all else fails, remember Rule 1.

Introduction

Principle comes first; action thereafter.

—Todd Stocker, speaker and pastor

The best place to start is at the beginning. We don't want you to search for or try to surmise the premise of this book.

Our premise:

Leading a team at a distance is first and foremost about leadership, and the principles of leadership haven't changed—they are principles. What has changed is that people are working in different places and perhaps at different times. Given those changes, how we apply the timeless principles of leadership in this new world matters a great deal—for the team members working at a distance, for you as their leader, and for the organization that you all serve.

This book is about both the principles and the nuances that matter so much.

While there are adjustments we need to make to lead in a world with more distance between team members, there is far more that won't change. We plan to show you the principles *and* nuances and help you recognize the difference.

This premise leaves us with a few things to clear up before we begin in earnest.

What Is Leadership?

More is being written about this topic than ever before, and still we need to set the context, since the words "leadership" and "leading" are both in the title of the book. Here is what we believe:

Leadership is present when people are choosing to follow someone toward a desired future outcome.

So . . . You are only leading if people are following.

There is a lot in those two short statements. Let us unpack it a bit more by sharing some truths and myths about leadership.

Leadership is complex

In visiting with leaders from NASA (a.k.a. rocket scientists), Kevin asked which was more complex—rocket science or leadership. The response was swift and simple—leadership was the clear and decisive winner. The group explained that in the world of building rockets, they can determine a right answer; they know the equations and formulas. They explained that if they put the right numbers into the right formulas at the right time (and check their math), they will get the right answer.

In visiting with leaders from NASA (a.k.a. rocket scientists), Kevin asked which was more complex—rocket science or leadership. The response was swift and simple—leadership was the clear and decisive winner.

But as a leader, you are dealing with *people*—and people are inherently more complex. And the issues, while perhaps not as dramatic as sending a rocket into orbit, are far more dynamic and are seldom black and white. Leadership isn't easy or simple. And, like rocket science, it is something that requires study and practice to become skilled. And when we add the complexity of leading people in different locations, it becomes even more complex.

Leadership is an action

Leadership is typically considered a role or a person, i.e., "They are the leader." While the dictionary says "leadership" is a noun, "leading," the actions that define leadership, is a verb. Leadership is not really something that we have or

2

possess; it is something that we *do*. When you think about leadership, think about actions and behaviors. The point of this book is to answer the question: What are the actions and behaviors that will help you help your teams (specifically remotely) get better results?

And if leadership is an action, that means it *isn't a title or position*. You are a leader when people follow you—if they aren't following, you aren't leading. The actions of others aren't guaranteed by a job title, the color of your desk, or the size of your office. A title that proclaims you a leader doesn't make you a leader any more than calling a lion a zebra creates black stripes.

Think of it this way: chances are you have observed or worked for a person with a leadership position who wasn't really leading. Alternatively, you know people who don't have or don't want the position, but people choose to follow them anyway. It is action, not titles, that makes leaders.

Leadership is a responsibility

When you were placed in or accepted a formal or informal role of leadership, you received a significant amount of responsibility. This may seem obvious if your title is president, CEO, or business owner, but your responsibility is massive as a first-level leader too. Think about it this way: outside of people's closest family and friends, you as their boss are about the most influential person in their life. You have an impact on their pay, their work environment (even if you aren't sitting in the same location), the level of stress they experience, the amount of satisfaction they find in their work, and a hundred other things.

People are looking to you. If you are leading, people are *following* you. You have a responsibility, therefore, for more than yourself and your own results. You must make sure that the direction you are headed is a useful and valuable one too. You can try to ignore this responsibility, but it won't change the significance of the role.

And while it is a responsibility, *it isn't a power grab*. The behaviors that lead to others granting you "power" don't come from you simply wanting it. They come from your relentless focus on serving others. If you try to grab power or claim authority, you aren't leading. When you lead in the ways we will discuss throughout this book, much "power" will likely be granted to you.

Leadership is an opportunity

Nothing positive happens in the world without leadership. The opportunity to make a difference is huge and exciting. Whether you are thinking about the difference you can make for your team, your customers, your organization at large, or the communities where you work and live, or even if you're thinking about changing the world, it all requires leadership.

When you exhibit the behaviors of leadership, you are actively trying to create new results that will make a difference in the world. Few things hold greater opportunity than this. Always remember that you have an opportunity to make a difference. Helping you make that difference with a far-flung team is a big reason why we wrote this book.

Leadership isn't a gift from birth

Leadership skills aren't doled out in the genetics of some while others are left wanting. All of us are given a unique bundle of DNA that can allow us to become highly effective, even remarkable leaders. Do some people have innate strengths that help them as leaders? Of course, but so do you—even if they are different strengths. None of that matters, though, if we don't do the things to use those strengths and do the things to improve in areas that are harder for us. Few things are sadder than unfulfilled potential. Leadership success isn't nearly as much about genetics as it is learning and improvement.

Leadership isn't management

The skills of management are focused on things: processes, procedures, plans, budgets, and forecasts. The skills of leadership focus on people, vision, influence, direction, and development. Both are valuable skill sets, and it is likely you need all these skills to be successful in your role. While not downplaying the management skills, recognize you are reading a book titled *The Long-Distance Leader*, not *The Long-Distance Manager*, and our focus will be on leadership throughout this book. The differences are clear but not distinct: think of the skill sets as overlapping circles, as seen in figure 1. We need to exhibit both sets of skills, but great leaders aren't necessarily great managers and vice versa.

4

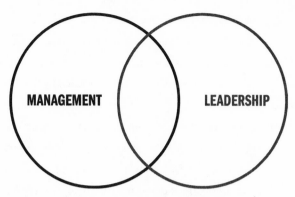

Figure 1   Two Parts of Your Role

To further make the point on the difference between leaders and managers, consider these lists.

Some Skills of Management

- Coordinating
- Planning
- Forecasting
- Budgeting
- Sourcing
- Directing
- Maintaining
- Problem solving
- Setting objectives
- Being tactical
- Focusing on the business
- Creating incremental improvement
- Doing things right
- Attending to details
- Focusing on processes

Some Skills of Leadership

- Collaborating
- Coaching
- Guiding
- Communicating
- Team building
- Creating change
- Providing vision
- Supporting
- Encouraging
- Setting goals
- Being strategic
- Creating purposeful disruption
- Doing the right things
- Thinking (and talking about) the big picture
- Focusing on people

While neither list is comprehensive, notice that all the behaviors in both lists are important, and to be at your best, you will have capability at all of them. Hopefully, though, the two lists make our point that the skills *are* different. This book will dive into some of the skills on the leadership list but few on the management list.

Remember, this book is about leading at a distance, which means we will talk about some critical leadership principles to provide context for what changes are necessary when leading remotely. This book isn't a complete treatise on leadership, so if you are looking for that, you are reading the wrong book. If you want or need more grounding on leadership principles, we recommend the books noted in the suggested reading list on page 195.

With this solid foundation, we are ready to get started. Let's start with what we have learned, and are learning, about Long-Distance Leaders.

Pause and Reflect

▶ What are your beliefs about leadership?

▶ What is your personal balance of skills between management and leadership?

Section One

Getting Started

Chapter 1

What We've Learned about Long-Distance Leaders

Rule 1: Think about leadership first, location second.

You cannot manage men into battle.
You manage things; you lead people.

—Admiral Grace Hopper

Eric is a solid manager and has had a traditional team in place for five years. Lately, he's been dealing with people working from home several days a week. On the surface everything's fine, but as he told us, he spends too much time worrying about what he doesn't know, or what might be happening, rather than the work itself. He second-guesses himself more than ever and feels less confident in his decisions. As he said, "So far so good, but for how long?" There are a lot of people like Eric.

If you're reading this, you agree with us that doing "okay" or "not terrible" isn't nearly good enough. Leadership is aspirational; no one who picked up this book wants to be merely average or normal. You want to be an excellent leader and, if possible, to achieve that with far less stress than you're experiencing now.

When we started looking at the day-to-day challenges faced by Long-Distance Leaders, we had a pretty good idea of what we'd find—after all, we've worked with dozens of organizations and thousands of people over the last few years. Still, we wanted to quantify what's happening in the world and check our assumptions with measurable data. That led to our Remote Leadership Survey.

In 2017, we conducted a voluntary survey of more than 225 managers who have at least part of their team working remotely.[1] Admittedly, this is a small sample size, but the results bear out what we're hearing every day. If we were looking for shocking results or data that came out of left field, we didn't find it. What we *did* discover is that the challenges for remote leaders very closely mirror those for managers in any situation, and that the majority of leaders report that things are . . . okay. Not perfect—things could always be better—but certainly not the-place-is-about-to-collapse awful either. There are also signs that as part-time teleworking increases and more companies change to a remote labor force, the cracks we did find will only grow.

The survey highlights challenges that arise because of the distance between people and the use of technology to bridge those gaps. As you'll see in a moment, that makes perfect sense, and it confirms that what we are experiencing with our clients isn't unusual. The data points out what needs to be done to prepare leaders for a new way to work and to help develop the skills required to do the job well.

Here is what we learned.

Demographics

- *The managers crossed every possible industry and discipline.* Government and sales accounted for 11 to 12 percent each, and even with seven categories, 46 percent of respondents were "other." This is an important point—leading remotely is a fact of life not limited to specific industries or disciplines.

- *The size of teams is changing.* Of the respondents surveyed, more than half had teams of ten people or more, 25 percent led two to five people, and 21 percent led six to ten people (figure 2). This is slightly more than the average of direct reports under the same roof and may indicate a new trend

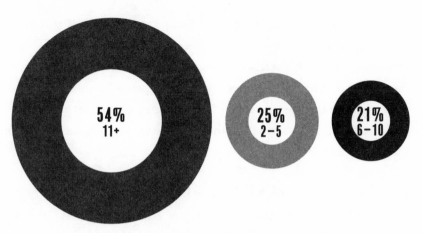

Figure 2   Sizes of Remote Teams

toward broader spans of control, which only exacerbates the challenges of leading remotely.

- *"Remote teams" doesn't mean everyone's working elsewhere.* We often think of remote teams as either wholly remote (everyone is scattered to the winds) or co-located. In fact, over 70 percent of leaders said they had a "hybrid" team, with a 50-50 split between teams with full-time and part-time remote employees. The other 30 percent had a completely or mostly remote team (figure 3). This is by far the fastest growing segment of the workforce. Failure to address this now means more stress down the road.

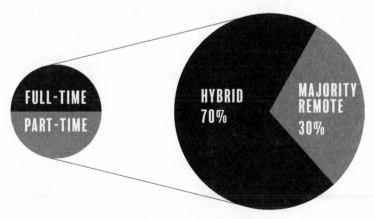

Figure 3   Team Makeup

- *Other demographic data.* Respondents were 60 percent male, 40 percent female, and they were an experienced bunch: 34 percent were aged forty to forty-nine and 37 percent were fifty to fifty-nine. A surprising 19 percent were over sixty. This makes sense since 78 percent of them had been managers for eight years or more. This confirms an important point: time as a leader doesn't seem to make the transition to long-distance leadership any easier.

What's Going On out There?

We reached a group of experienced managers, across multiple industries. Yet when we asked, "How's it going?" the answers were strangely in accord. Here are some examples:

- Over half say they "get the job done," and an additional 28 percent say their team is "highly productive."

- When asked, "Where do the productivity challenges lie?" 10 percent say the problems are with remote members, 4 percent say they are with the "home team," and 69 percent say there's no pattern to it or it's hard to identify the roots of the problems.

- Trust runs a little below productivity, and while most managers say the level of trust is okay (both between themselves and individuals, and between the various members of the team), there are more problems reported here than anywhere else on the survey. The largest part of our respondents say that trust levels aren't awful, but it's a gap worth working on.

The Biggest Worries

Finally, we asked specific questions about challenges these leaders face. We presented four common questions remote leaders often ask themselves and The feedback we received is shown in figure 4.

The first question gets asked most frequently when working remotely is new, or in organizations or industries where trust is traditionally low, including highly regulated union environments and government. Based on our experience, senior leadership is overly worried about precisely what people are

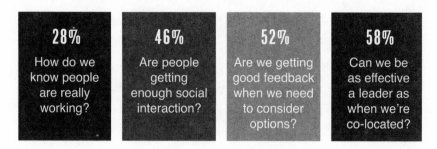

Figure 4   The Biggest Worries

doing at any given time. Notice that remote leaders are more worried about the last three questions, which are more personal.

What Are People Afraid of?

On the surface, it sounds as if everything is generally fine. You have experienced people feeling pretty good about the people they lead, and the work is getting done. What's the problem? But when you explore the written comments, you see the cracks in the armor, and they echo the concerns we hear every day.

- "With people around the world, it's become impossible to 'turn off.' I'm connected 24/7/365."

- "We aren't efficient at meetings. Too many people check out or don't participate."

- "There are divisions between the remote people and those who work in the office."

- "We don't see many engagement or performance challenges until it's too late."

- "We're great at getting work done that's properly defined and scoped. It's coming up with new ideas, dealing with surprises, or implementing new things that create problems."

- "Focusing on the urgent vs. the important is hard enough, but you don't know what others are focused on."

We could go on, of course, and we'll share more comments and stories as we go, but here's what the data says to us.

- Leaders are making things happen in this new environment because they are working longer and harder. They want to succeed in the virtual world, but they're doing it through effort and guesswork. We believe there is a better way.

- Although many organizations are starting to plan for teleworking (with policies and support) and training their remote leaders, the planning lags behind the reality. Leaders are trusting their instincts and doing the best they can, yet they aren't finding the support they need in existing company training or general business literature.

- They lack confidence in themselves. Phrases like "I'm never sure . . ." or "I worry about . . ." pepper the comments. This uncertainty undermines effectiveness and adds to the stress of a new and unfamiliar work landscape.

- Experienced leaders sometimes struggle with technology. As psychologist Jean Twenge says in her book *iGen*, experienced leaders are used to a different way of working.[2] Though many of the things that enabled their success are still relevant, there's a feeling that they're working with one hand tied behind their backs and struggling to connect with younger, more tech-savvy employees.

- Generally, those new to leadership roles are comfortable with technology but lack fundamental leadership skills.

Some Important Things to Remember

As you read through the rest of this book, here are some important things to think about:

- Remote leadership, while becoming far more common, has always existed. It can be done well, and you can do it.

- Leading at a distance is still leading—and while there is far more that has remained the same, the differences must be acknowledged and addressed to have the success you want and your team deserves.

- The skills you need to communicate, influence, build strong working relationships, and engage people can be learned, developed, and replicated throughout the organization, but only if you understand the dynamics at work and identify the skill gaps to mindfully address them.
- It's not just you. The very questions, doubts, and concerns that brought you to this book are simultaneously challenging millions of other smart, talented, dedicated—and exhausted—leaders.

Pause and Reflect

▶ What are your biggest concerns or challenges about leading at a distance?

Online Resource

If you'd like to take the survey for yourself, go to

http://RemoteLeadershipInstitute.com/LDLsurvey

and add to the data we're collecting to help other future leaders.

Chapter 2

How We Got to Long-Distance Leadership

Rule 2: Accept the fact that leading remotely requires you to lead differently.

Uneasy lies the head that wears a crown.

—Henry the IV, Part 2 by William Shakespeare

Being a leader has never been a simple task. The struggle to be effective, to achieve your (and your organization's) goals, and help the people you lead reach their destination is constant. It's a challenge, and you've accepted, so get on with it.

Patty is one of those leaders. She's worked with the same team for three years, with everyone in the same location, and a big part of everyone's social activity revolves around work. Two years ago, people were allowed to work from home if necessary—snowstorms, sick kids—but now half the team is out of the office at least three days a week. There is no plan, no standardized processes, and her training has always involved face-to-face communication over everything else. Also, she's not terribly fond of technology and relies too much on email. As a result, she's holding off communicating until everyone's all together, but that is leaving some people out of the loop or with information that isn't timely. It's frustrating, and she has asked us, "How did this happen?"

It's easy to discount the challenges of the way the workplace works today, especially the impact of distance and technology-enabled communication, and just focus on what has always made leaders effective. After all, Genghis Khan ruled half the known world and never held a single WebEx meeting. The sun never set on Queen Victoria's British Empire, yet there's no recorded instance of a single conference call. It's not like others haven't done it before us, and there is no reason we can't do it more effectively, productively, and with less stress. Discounting or diminishing the problems doesn't change the fact that there's been a fundamental change both in the way people work together and how leaders are expected to communicate. As Patty has noticed, and her company has yet to address, this change has had a profound impact on leadership behavior, attitudes, and results.

When Genghis had to communicate an order, there were real live people in front of him, professional clerks who carefully wrote down his words and then passed those commands on down the line. When you need to communicate change order to your project team, how often do you stare out at a sea of empty desks (or the strangers in the Starbucks where you are working) tapping out instructions on your phone, wondering if the team will understand and heed the directive?

It may have always been lonely at the top, but now we're literally, physically, by ourselves much of the time. When Queen Victoria grumbled, "We are not amused," the person she was scolding stood in front of her and knew she meant it. They couldn't slough it off with an "LOL" and a shrug emoji.

In fact, the world of work has changed a lot in the last quarter century or so. Here are some of the ways it used to be:

- *The number of managers, team leaders, and others who sent their own written correspondence was very low.* Above a certain level in most organizations, letters and documents were created by assistants, clerks, or other trained professionals. At the very least, such communication was checked by someone else before going out into the world. You didn't (and couldn't) simply hit "send" or "reply all."

- *Email didn't exist for most people.* Some of us can remember our first email accounts. We couldn't access them except by computer (usually at work), and there was no guarantee that your intended audience had access to that tool either. Now it's probably the number one form of business communication (and the most complained about).

- *Most business communication that wasn't face-to-face was done on the telephone.* Less than fifteen years ago, the percentage of time people spent talking on the telephone outweighed the time spent reading and writing email significantly. Now the time spent on those activities has reversed, and the trend continues.

- *Most team leaders, supervisors, and managers had the people they worked with in a single location, or within easy physical reach.* Only leaders at the regional level and above in large companies had to worry about managing people remotely. Leadership development and training assumed a lot of face-to-face contact. That may not match your reality today, and most leaders say they haven't received sufficient (or any) training in the real dynamics of leading remote and hybrid teams.

And there is more that has changed over that twenty-five years . . .

- Today, according to the Project Management Institute, 90 percent of project teams have at least one member (usually more) who aren't co-located with the rest of the team.[1]

- An increasing number of project teams and task forces are made up of people who don't report to the same manager. The leaders of these matrixed teams must influence and lead people without being their boss or having traditional reporting relationships.

- Today, nearly 80 percent of white-collar supervisors have at least one direct report who works in a different location—at least part-time.[2] This includes everyone from colleagues on the other side of the world to a team member who has decided to work from home one day because of the weather. Either way, they aren't sitting within arm's reach of you or each other.

- Social media and electronic communication have changed how information (or disinformation) spreads, and how quickly. It used to be that responding to a request took at least enough time to dip the quill in ink and handwrite a response, drop it in an envelope, and ship it across the ocean. Or the person communicated with you directly.

The important thing about all these numbers is that it drives home how much things have changed in terms of how we do our jobs. There are two major repercussions for leaders as a result:

- The communication methods that enabled us to succeed (if we've been around for a while) have changed. You may be terrific in a face-to-face meeting . . . but how many of those will you have today? Maybe you're a great listener, but if Bob in Dallas only communicates with you through email, that strength is negated, and it begs the question whether the two of you are really working as effectively as you could and should.

- The notion of a leader's sense of isolation is no longer simply emotional. You're not only lonely because you have the sole responsibility for decisions, or the weight of authority, or feel responsible if people lose their jobs—you're often actually physically alone.

First, you need to cut yourself some slack. After all, if you've been doing this job for a long time, the things you're expected to do and the tools you're expected to use have changed considerably in a short period of time. If you're new to the role of leader, chances are the people who mentor and teach you aren't familiar with working the same way you do. This is still largely uncharted territory.

Before, when you made a decision, asked a question, or gave direction, you looked in the other person's face, or at least heard their voice. You could tell if you were understood or if they agreed with what you were saying. You had real-time feedback so you could coach, answer questions, or change course quickly. If you needed answers, you got them immediately. You even occasionally got a smile or a "thank you" that made you feel good. These are just some of the real emotional rewards that can come with being an effective leader.

But now, some of the rewards may be missing. Like Patty, it feels as if you're working in the dark, unsure what's happening, operating largely on faith (even when you don't have much), and doing it all in ways we and our predecessors have never done before.

One of our clients put it this way: "Managing has always felt like herding cats. But now I'm trying to herd cats by email."

Before we get caught up in how things are different and how much things have changed, let's take a breath. The truth is that while there have been significant changes to the way we lead, the act of *leadership* itself hasn't really changed all that much.

"Managing has always felt like herding cats. But now I'm trying to herd cats by email."

This is a first-order change, not a second. What's the difference? A first-order change means we need *to do the same things but in a different way.* We need to do something faster, smarter, using different tools, but the task at hand is fundamentally the same. A second-order change implies what we're doing doesn't work at all, and we need to do something completely different.

Here's an example. Let's say one of your team members is chronically late to work. There are plenty of ways you can help them address this problem: they can leave home fifteen minutes earlier, change their route to work, or even agree to stay fifteen minutes later each day so they're putting in the same amount of work. Those are all first-order changes.

If those solutions don't work, you might work to accommodate their needs, or suggest they find a new job. That's a second-order change: how you're doing things isn't working, so you need to change what you do.

Being a Long-Distance Leader may feel radically different from how you've worked in the past. Maybe you were more comfortable when you shared an office space with your coworkers or got to see them face-to-face more often than you do now. Those changes may be creating emotional stress that impacts your productivity and how effective you can be.

What you do may not be the problem, but how you do it may well be. In the next section, we'll share a model that helps illustrate that fact.

Pause and Reflect

▶ What has been the biggest change in the way your team works over the last year? If you're new and don't have a good answer, what is the biggest change you've noticed from the way your previous bosses handled the job?

▶ Have you noticed any changes in your leadership behavior because of working separately from your people? If so, what are they?

▶ What is the most stressful part of leading people who work apart from you?

▶ What is working well? What do you know for sure is not working well?

Chapter 3

What It Means to Lead at a Distance

Rule 3: Know that working remotely changes the interpersonal
dynamics, even if you don't want it to.

Sometimes when I consider what tremendous consequences come from
little things . . . I am tempted to think . . . there are no little things.

—Bruce Barton, ad executive and US congressman

Ahmed had been a supervisor for a couple of years, but all of his team was right down the hall. With a corporate policy change, three of his team members are now working from home. He knows the world has changed but doesn't really understand what that will mean for him and what he must do each day. He's often surprised at how little misunderstandings turn into problems and how people miss messages he thought were perfectly clear.

In this chapter, we are going to talk more about the distance that Ahmed (and you) are experiencing and what it all means. We are going to expand on the last chapter to make sure you know where you are and where you want to go.

The title of this book seems simple enough. A Long-Distance Leader is someone who leads from a physical location separate from at least some of the people he or she leads. That covers a lot of situations, though, based on the way the modern workplace works.

Remote vs. Virtual

Here's some basic terminology that will be important as we continue. First, there's the issue of "remote" teams and "virtual" teams. They are used interchangeably but aren't necessarily the same.

According to Dr. Karen Sobel Lojeski,[1] formerly of Stonybrook University (SUNY Stonybrook) and now CEO of Virtual Distance International, here's the distinction: Remote distance is just what it says. The people you lead are somewhere else at least part of the time. Perhaps you're a sales manager with people working from the road who are constantly on their laptops and phones. Or you're a project lead with team members scattered from Bangor to Bangalore. Or the company you run has a single location, but you have one person who, because of childcare needs, works from home one day a week.

The important thing about these teams is that team members may not be in physical proximity to each other. They lack the constant visual and other cues that frequent interaction and exposure to each other provide. Communication might be constantly mediated by screens and email. Meanwhile, the reporting structure and the power balance is fairly traditional. Things are different, but it's to a much lesser degree than it feels at first.

Virtual distance is more complicated. Communication is primarily through technology, and you may be separated by distance, but there are structural differences to the relationship. If you lead a project where your team is made up of people from different departments, for example, you may have all the responsibility of a leader but none of the actual authority. Project teams and ad hoc teams are frequently "virtual"; there's a project manager or leader, but that person may have no direct supervisory power—everyone on the team has a "real boss" they report to. This makes influence, rather than authority, the main way to get things done. The traditional levers of power ("I'm the boss, you have to do what I say") aren't as simple as in the past. It's hard to twist arms through a phone line.

Additionally, virtual distance can be emotional. If you have a coworker who would rather send you an email than actually talk to you, there is virtual distance, even though the "remote distance" is easily covered. Now imagine they are literally out of sight (they couldn't walk to your office if they wanted to)—how much more difficult would it be?

Types of Teams

We also need to be clear about what we mean when we talk about team dynamics. Whether it's a functional team, a project team, or a political campaign, there are three types of teams a leader today might work with:

- *Co-located teams.* Here everyone's working in the same location the vast majority of the time. This is the kind of team most of us grew up on.

- *Completely remote teams.* People work together toward a common goal, but they do most of their work physically separated from each other. Most communication then will not be face-to-face. A classic example is a sales manager with one direct report per region.

- *Hybrid teams.* Some of your people share a workspace; others are in other locations. This might include full-time teleworkers, people in other offices, or even those working on a client site. A subset of the hybrid team is when people work from home a couple of days a week—or whenever they feel like it. If you've ever held a meeting with some people in a conference room and others dialing in on a speakerphone, you know there are some unique challenges. One of the fastest-changing challenges for hybrid teams is that people are constantly changing where they work—sometimes they're in the office, sometimes they're away—so processes and access to information can change almost daily. Your team might be a hybrid, with most people in the office one day, then completely virtual the next.

Each of these types of teams has things in common (they need to get work done, exchange information, and build on each other's work) and unique challenges (management by walking around doesn't work if you are in Seattle and part of your team is in Sydney or Singapore). But our focus will be on completely remote and hybrid teams through this book.

Beyond these distinctions, there are further differences for your remote or hybrid teams, based on the context of the work. Consider the following:

- *Sales teams.* If you have a team of salespeople, it is likely that you once were one of those salespeople. Sales teams have been doing the remote thing longer, which can mean they experience less pain working remotely, or as we have often found it just means they don't know how much better it could be. They have accepted the issues and difficulties of working remotely.

- *Project or ad hoc teams.* These teams may be shorter lived, with high-stakes results on the line. You might be leading a project team and not have some (or any) of the team members reporting to you.

- *Individual contributor teams.* Sales teams likely fall into this category, but they aren't the only example. When you lead a team of individual contributors, the focus on remote teamwork and collaboration might not be as strong, yet you still must keep them from becoming too insulated or individually minded. They are still on a team, with team goals and objectives.

- *Global teams.* At some point if people aren't in the building, it doesn't matter how far away they are . . . except where cultural differences and vast differences in time zones make communication and relationship building more challenging.

What Hasn't Changed

Kevin has had this question on his whiteboard for several months: *"How does leadership change, and what shouldn't change?"* In many ways that sums up this section of the book, and it certainly is the focus of this chapter.

First, here's what shouldn't change . . .

- *The leader's primary focus.* Whether they are outside your office door, down the hall, out in the warehouse, or in another time zone or country, leadership is still about human beings. Too often leaders want to move to the details of situation or context without first remembering that team members have feelings, emotions, needs, and personal objectives that need to be considered. Start with the idea that everything starts with people and you will start in the right place.

- *The fundamentals of human behavior.* Since you are leading people, the more you understand the psychology of people—their wants, needs, desires, fears, and anxieties—the more successful you will be. Contrary to what you might read in the popular or trendy business press, the fundamentals of human behavior have not changed because people work from a different location, use a certain type of technology, or were born in a certain year. We will point to these fundamentals throughout the book.

- *The principles of leadership.* Along with the fundamentals of human behavior, there are skills and characteristics that lead people to follow some people more than others. These traits, characteristics, and skills haven't changed as people have migrated from the office to their homes or a client location.

- *The roles of leaders.* Regardless of where the team is located, leaders are asked to coach, influence, and communicate. They are expected to coalesce and collaborate with teams, set goals, and lead change. We talked a bit about this in chapter 1, but it deserves a reminder here: the basic roles expected of leaders haven't changed as the team has dispersed.

- *The high-level expectations of our output.* Our organizations still want us to hit production targets, finish valuable projects, meet a budget, work safely, and a hundred other things. These high-level work goals don't change when people work in different places.

While those important things haven't changed, we must recognize and address the differences caused by distance or, like Ahmed, we'll experience frustration and unexpected surprises.

What Has Changed

You're reading this book because something has changed dramatically in the way you work. Odds are, it's one or more of the following.

Geography

We've worked with organizations that talk about leading teams on different floors or different buildings on the same corporate campuses. There is no doubt that some of the long-distance factors we will discuss in this book are valid even over short distance. What is changing is how geographically dispersed we have become. Kevin has for many years led a team spread across seventy-five miles, but now that team spans from Richmond, Virginia, to Chicago, to Phoenix, to Fort Wayne, to Indianapolis and beyond. Even that isn't as dispersed as many of you face, with teams spanning the globe from Dallas, Texas, to Dubai; from Dublin to Danforth, Illinois. These geographic changes matter, perhaps in different ways than you initially might think.

Now you don't just have distance but time zones, cultural norms and expectations, and generally more complexity to your work as a leader . . . as if it wasn't complicated enough.

You are out of sight

This may seem obvious, but when leading at a distance you aren't seen as often by the people you want to influence.

If you want to lead by example, it is much easier if people can see you. If you want others to help each other, they need to see you are willing to roll up your sleeves yourself—after all, if you aren't above doing the dirty work, people will notice. Those physically around can see that your behavior is consistent with your values.

When you share space with people, they can ask questions on the fly or request a meeting at a moment's notice because your door is open or they know you are around. People not in the office can't have that awareness, so you must have processes to overcome this difference.

As strange as it feels at first, your physical presence conveys the power of your position and your willingness to lead. If people need to schedule time with you, aren't sure if now is a good time to ask a question, or haven't developed a warm personal relationship with you, you have both immediate and long-term problems to overcome.

Whether we're talking actual physical presence or "virtual presence" where you are available and visible to your people, "being seen" is critical to leadership and suffers in a long-distance relationship.

Technology

Kevin started his company with a fax machine and internet through CompuServe. Besides letting you know that Kevin has been around awhile, it reminds us how much the world of technology has changed and will continue to change. Recognizing the technology available to you and using it appropriately and effectively can be a big lever for your success as a Long-Distance Leader. Keeping up with new tools that make your work and communication more effective is part of your job.

If you aren't using the available tools, your team won't either. And if you aren't using them well, the resistance will increase. If they don't have a model of success because you aren't using the tools well or at all, good luck getting them to use those tools.

If you are a Long-Distance Leader, and perhaps especially if you are of our generation, this means you must encourage the use of the right tools at the right times, and you must use them yourself.

Working Relationships

Although people aren't working in the same building or corridor, they still work together, hand off work to each other, and therefore must communicate successfully.

And although relationships don't develop or improve simply because of regular face-to-face interaction, personal contact provides a boost in creating working relationships. So, the need for working relationships (both practically and psychologically) doesn't change when people work remotely from each other, but the opportunities and context for building those relationships changes drastically. Learning how to build and maintain them is always an important part of your work as a leader.

And . . . *virtual communication changes the interpersonal dynamic, even if you don't want it to.* As a Long-Distance Leader, it gets harder—and perhaps even more important—to intentionally nurture relationships with all your team members.

You get fewer communication cues

When you speak to someone face-to-face, you get instantaneous feedback. Some of it is purposeful—people can ask questions or comment, and as a leader you should encourage honest responses to your messages. Much of this is involuntary; the broad smile of acceptance or the furrowing of a brow tells us we need to adjust our message, repeat it, check for understanding, or get more information before we proceed. We constantly and naturally adjust our messages on the fly based on those real-time responses.

When working at a distance, the balance of communication modes changes. Think about how much of your interaction takes place in writing. Email, texts, and online communication are your most frequent methods of passing information back and forth. That often feels impersonal and cold. It's one-way communication and demands that you hone all your communication skills, not just your verbal ones.

When we do speak, it's on the phone—with only our tone of voice and words and without the supporting evidence of smiles, winks, or posture to help support our message. And even when people can see us (if we're using webcams or videoconferencing), there is a conscious separation from our audience that video alone can't completely overcome.

In a world where those immediate cues are missing, you must ensure your message is easily understood and that you find other ways to receive critical cues. Sure, you sent that email saying you're changing how the process for the Jackson account is going to work. But does that mean people really have the information they need to change or know how this will impact them? Are they blithely accepting the news, or are they freaking out and frantically instant messaging each other while you sit back thinking everything's fine?

We have all spent a lifetime learning to communicate in person—and now we're conducting our most important work in ways that we may be less effective and comfortable with.

Information gets filtered

The way information is received is often filtered and mediated in unexpected or unintended ways.

As a leader, you don't just send messages; you receive them . . . in mass quantities and multiple forms. When you work in proximity with people, you can pop in for a clarifying chat or watch their body language as they give you bad news and respond accordingly. When you receive information on the phone, often without context or advance notice, it is hard to make sure you're really reading carefully, processing the information clearly, and responding in ways you are proud of.

Your approach to leadership may be out of date

For a lot of us, our first leadership experiences occurred where everyone was in the same location. We could walk through the cube farm and see who was (or at least appeared to be) working and who wasn't. We overheard conversations or saw actions and could respond proactively and immediately.

Like us, you may have had managers or leaders who relied on the old "command and control" method of getting things done ("Because I said so"). Because they were nearby or could pop in at any moment, they watched everything we did and made sure we did it exactly the way they wanted it done. Whether that was good or bad, it was at least *possible*.

But when your team is scattered to the far corners of the continent, it is impossible to know what every person is doing all the time. Even if you wanted to monitor absolutely everything they do and make sure people weren't slacking off, you couldn't do it, and it's important to ask why you'd even want to. Since you can't know exactly what everyone's doing at any given time, you need to find ways to make sure people have the proper guidance for their tasks, are clear on the metrics, and their progress is communicated to you in ways that give you what you need to maintain progress—and your sanity. Stated another way, to lead successfully at a distance you must build greater trust with your team members—command and control won't work and will drive you crazy trying.

(Some of) people's needs change

The basic needs of humans don't change, but the context of working locations may make some needs more important or obvious than they were in the past. If you have team members teleworking from their home, they may have interaction needs that were previously met in the workplace that now are missing. As a Long-Distance Leader, you must notice the needs that surface and find ways to help meet them. Why? Because as those needs are met, people are better able to focus on and complete their work successfully.

As a Long-Distance Leader, it gets harder—and perhaps even more important—to intentionally nurture relationships with all your team members.

This isn't only true for the more extroverted on your team who especially might miss the interaction and flow of life at the office while working remotely. In this digitally connected world, people have become increasingly isolated from each other physically, and the workplace has been for many that oasis of connection. Now, as people work from home, we as leaders must be aware of these needs. If we help people meet those needs and encourage them to do so, we get not only more productive team members but healthier and less stressed ones too.

More individual work focus

Often as people work remotely, their work becomes more focused on individual tasks and individual contributions. This shift to an individual focus and away from "the team" isn't necessarily bad; in some cases, it probably leads to better results. It is, however, a change that needs to be recognized by the organization, by us as leaders, and perhaps most importantly by the individuals doing the work. Recognizing this focus and making it overt—and at the same time not inadvertently individualizing the focus too much—is a nuance worth noting.

Working in isolation

Leading at a distance is literally a lonely job.

While it's lovely to have uninterrupted time to get your w⟨
the joy of leadership is being with other people. Hearing oth⟨
ting timely answers to questions, brainstorming, and building on ideas is an
exciting part of your role.

But where do you turn when you have a simple question? Do you have
access to trusted advisors when you experience doubt? Can you check your
assumptions, or do you come up with an idea and fire off orders without running them by someone close by first? Moreover, you don't get to see the acceptance of your ideas or hear good news firsthand . . . never mind being able to
celebrate over pizza or a slice of birthday cake in the break room.

Our survey confirms that feeling isolated from their teams is a huge concern for leaders and impacts their effectiveness and job satisfaction. But who
are you supposed to turn to for information, inspiration, and companionship
in an increasingly long-distance workplace?

Now What?

Yes, being a Long-Distance Leader is difficult. It's also not impossible.
(Remember, Genghis Khan and Queen Victoria did it . . . so can you.) You
have to think about your job in new ways, be aware of the changing dynamics
that impact you and your work, and change some behaviors.

In the rest of this book we'll look at each of the challenges we face as leaders, how leading at a distance affects them, and the new attitudes, points of
view, and behaviors we'll have to apply to these changes.

Pause and Reflect

▶ What type of team do you have, and how does that inform how you lead?

▶ How has distance changed the way your team works and your effectiveness?

▶ How has working apart from people changed your approach to leadership?

▶ Which of the changes are impacting you the most?

Section Two

Models That Matter

Chapter 4

The Remote Leadership Model

Rule 4: Use technology as a tool, not as a barrier or an excuse.

All the tools, techniques, and technology in the world are nothing without the head, heart, and hands to use them wisely, kindly, and mindfully.

—Rasheed Ogunlaru, speaker and coach

Alan has been leading successfully for a long time. When the company allowed some team members to work from home and then changed the org chart so he had some folks in the Mobile plant reporting to him, neither he nor his boss thought much about it. He knew all the players and they knew him, he knew the work, and he knew how to lead. When IT gave him access to some new technology, he thought, "I don't need that, I have all the tools I need, it's working fine."

So, if being a leader in a remote environment isn't *really* all that different, why does it feel lonelier, more stressful, and just plain harder?

After a lot of thought and discussion with remote leaders, we came up with a simple model that conveys a big message. We call it the Remote Leadership Model (figure 5).

The model depicts three interworking gears that work together to propel remote work forward. The largest gear is "Leadership & Management," which is

LEADERSHIP
& MANAGEMENT

SKILL &
IMPACT

TOOLS &
TECHNOLOGY

Figure 5   The Remote Leadership Model

the work you were hired to do. The second smaller but critical gear is the "Tools & Technology" you must use in order to make the work happen at distance. Finally, the smallest gear is "Skill & Impact"—the ability to use those tools well. Although it is the smallest gear, you can't ignore it or dismiss its importance.

Let's break it down further.

The Leadership and Management Gear

This gear reminds us that our job as leaders—the leadership and management behaviors we are expected to exhibit—are the same as they've ever been. *What* we're supposed to do (the expectations) haven't changed much since the project manager at the pyramids plied his craft. Regardless of whether our people share a cube farm or are scattered around the globe, these are the things expected of leaders.

In his book *Remarkable Leadership*, Kevin outlined thirteen competencies that apply to all leaders. To improve in your effectiveness, you must continue to develop in these competency areas:

1. Remarkable leaders learn continually.

2. Remarkable leaders champion change.

3. Remarkable leaders communicate powerfully.

4. Remarkable leaders build relationships.

5. Remarkable leaders develop others.

6. Remarkable leaders focus on customers.

7. Remarkable leaders influence with impact.

8. Remarkable leaders think and act innovatively.

9. Remarkable leaders value collaboration and teamwork.

10. Remarkable leaders solve problems and make decisions.

11. Remarkable leaders take responsibility and are accountable.

12. Remarkable leaders manage projects and processes successfully.

13. Remarkable leaders set goals and support goal achievement.

You can quibble about the list, or whether something does or doesn't belong there, or how to label the competencies, but you can't argue that working remotely makes any of those behaviors less important. Furthermore, leading remotely doesn't add much to this rather imposing menu. The job of leading remains the same whether you're all together or not. The work needs to be done, whether people are outside your office door or in Guam.

How well you've demonstrated your abilities in those areas is another question for another time, but until recently we've only ever had to really perform our duties in a centuries-old way: together in the same place, and pretty much face-to-face. This is no longer the case.

The difference lies in the other two gears. Smaller doesn't mean insignificant; the old expression "little hinges swing big doors" is as true now as it's ever been.

The Tools and Technology Gear

This intermediary gear is perhaps the most important difference when leading remotely. Leaders are expected to exhibit all the leadership behaviors we've mentioned, and do it using tools and technology with which they might not be comfortable. That's a bigger deal than you might think.

If you're an American and have ever driven in England, you've probably risked your life proving this point. At first blush, driving a car is driving a car:

four wheels, steering wheel, combustion engine, windshield in the front—it's more than 90 percent the same as driving in your own neighborhood. The only differences are that the steering wheel is on the other side of the car and you drive on the other side of the road.

These "small differences" have led to an awful lot of stressful drives and near misses. And it's not just driving. Even walking is impacted by the direction of traffic. The city of London has painted arrows on the streets that basically say, "Hey Stupid Tourist, the bus is coming from the other way—watch where you step." It's a small change that can mean the difference between a carefree vacation and a visit to the emergency room.

How does technology impact your leadership behavior? You likely feel those differences every time you want to ask a complex question but settle for sending an email, or when you know you should have a critical coaching session and make do having it on the telephone (where you can't see the happy gleam in the other person's eye or the panicked look on their face). Making a presentation via webinar technology isn't nearly as rewarding as being at the front of an assembled crowd, gaining energy through the audience's laughter and applause.

This gear begs three important questions.

- What tools do you have at your disposal to help get the job done?

- Are you using the right tool for the right job?

- Do you rely too much on the tools you're comfortable with?

As with so much in life, using the wrong tool for the job can be frustrating and diminish your effectiveness. That matters because you have a demanding job as a leader, with a lot of things that need to go right. You don't want to be "driving on the wrong side of the road." That certainly makes things more complicated, but that's not the only problem.

The Skill and Impact Gear

The third (and smallest) gear is the simplest concept, the easiest one to maintain, yet often the one that can cause the biggest problems. Having a clear idea of what you should do is important, and choosing the appropriate tool for that job is critical. But if you can't use the tool you've chosen effectively, all the hard work and good intentions in the world won't get the job done.

Here are some important statistics:

- Software developers are aware of a rule of thumb that applies to nearly every software tool ever built—80 percent of people use 20 percent of the features.[1] Having a robust tool like WebEx or Skype for Business doesn't help you overcome the challenges of remote communication if you don't use the features available to you.

- Two MIT Sloan–Cap Gemini Studies show that leaders who use and are comfortable with technology are rated consistently higher in other leadership areas than those who don't. Yet a huge number—a big majority— don't feel comfortable or confident using the tools themselves.[2]

- In numerous off-the-record, private conversations, both the people who work for well-known software platforms and their resellers have told us the same story. Two-thirds or more of the people who get licenses for web-meeting tools never receive any training or coaching, apart from online tutorials, which many people find extremely unsatisfactory. As one reseller put it, "It's like, 'Here's your _____ license. Try not to hurt someone.'"

Not only do we have tools with which we're unfamiliar, we're not using them well. That can undermine our credibility and effectiveness. This is true for anyone trying to communicate today, but for leaders there are additional challenges:

- Leaders are usually more senior in age and/or experience to those they lead and therefore might be more resistant to adopting new technology, or at least they are uncomfortable with it at first.

- Even if you want to adopt technology, odds are you are behind the learning curve compared to those you work with/lead.

- The paradox is that if you don't use the tools, you look out of touch and incompetent, but you don't adopt the technology because you are afraid of looking incompetent and uncomfortable.

The Remote Leadership Model shows that long-distance leadership is a difficult job where it's hard to excel. You are being asked to do your job in ways you've never done it before, using tools you aren't confident in your ability to succeed with. The lesson of the Remote Leadership Model is simple: the job of leading—*what we do*—hasn't changed nearly as much as *how we do it*.

For the rest of the book, we'll be constantly drawing distinctions between how leading has always been done in the past with how you need to think and act in today's workplace, because that's what's really changed for us all.

Pause and Reflect

▶ Take a moment to look at the Remote Leadership Model and ask yourself these questions:

▶ How comfortable are you with the Leadership and Management gear? On a scale of 1 to 5 (Not Very Effective to Very Effective), what areas from the lists on page 38 and 39 do you feel you excel in? What areas require growth?

▶ How comfortable are you with the Tools and Technology gear? On a scale of 1 to 5, what tools are aiding your communication and work (e.g., Skype, WebEx, Dropbox)? Which seem to get in the way or do not offer much help?

▶ Think of a time when you ignored or didn't use a technology and now you wish you had. What happened, and why would you do it differently next time?

▶ How comfortable are with the Skill and Impact gear? On a scale of 1 to 5, how confident and competent are you using communication technology?

▶ Based on these answers, what new skills would you like to develop that will help you be a more effective Long-Distance Leader?

Chapter 5

The Three O Model of Leadership

Rule 5: Leading requires a focus on outcomes, others, and ourselves.

The greatest leader is not necessarily the one who does the greatest things. He is the one that gets the people to do the greatest things.

—Ronald Reagan

Connie is a new project manager with a team scattered across the Americas. She's a leader who is getting the job done but starting to feel the stress of working beyond her comfort zone. Though her project is on time and on budget, she is starting her day earlier in order to accommodate stakeholders in Asia and scheduling meetings after her children's bedtime. While the team seems to be doing fine, she is tired, cranky, and fears she can't maintain this pace for long. "If this is what leadership is," she asked us, "how long can someone keep it up?"

How would you define or describe leadership?

For many years, Kevin has done an exercise with groups that is both instructive and inspirational. He starts by asking people to individually *define or describe leadership in exactly six words.* Without fail, no matter the location or experience of the groups, two fundamental points come through. The most common understanding is that leadership is about:

- *outcomes* (stated with such words as "goals," "mission," "vision," "objectives," and "success")

- *other* people (stated with such words as "influencing," "coaching," "communicating," and "building teams")

The good news is that people generally agree on what good leadership looks like regardless of where they live and work. Facilitating this exercise over the years has had a profound impact on Kevin and his philosophy about leadership—even though in every case he has been the supposed expert on the topic. It is from his experience, as well as leading this exercise with people from around the world, that we developed the Three O Model of Leadership (figure 6).

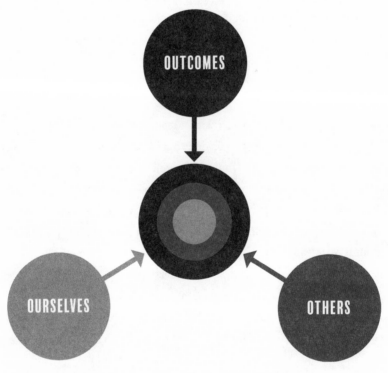

Figure 6   The Three O Model of Leadership

As you can see from the figure, the Three O Model of Leadership outlines *three* areas of focus all leaders must recognize and use to reach their maximum success.

- *Outcomes*—you lead people with the purpose of reaching a desired outcome.

- *Others*—you lead with and through other people to reach those outcomes.

- *Ourselves*—you can't leave yourself out of this model. While leadership is about outcomes and other people, none of that happens without you whether you like it or not.

In the story at the beginning of this chapter, Connie was very sensitive to the first two O's. While Outcomes and Others must come first, leaders must also pay attention to the Ourselves part of the model to successfully lead others to the desired outcomes. For all kinds of positive reasons, she was not supporting herself, and that's where the cracks began to appear in both her confidence and competence.

This model is a more complete picture of the biggest gear in the Remote Leadership Model we shared with you in the last chapter.

Like all models, our Three O Model provides a way to clarify and compartmentalize a far more complex world and allows us to prioritize our thoughts and actions. But we believe this is not just a behavioral model but a mindset.

To lead at your best, you must think of the Outcomes and Others components first. Although the Ourselves component sits in the center of our model, this doesn't imply that you are the center of leadership, nor the purpose for it. You are at the core, not the center. Leadership doesn't revolve around you; rather, you bring who you are and how you lead to bear on creating better outcomes for others. This model is meant to show you that while none of this is *about* you, you can't be taken out of the equation either. (Many would call this "servant leadership,"[1] and whether you use that language or not, our belief is none of us can lead in a sustainably successful way without being a servant to others and outcomes.) And while leadership isn't about you, who you are, what you believe, and how you behave are critical to your success.

Now that we have described the model at a high level and put it in proper perspective, let's dive into each of the O's.

Figure 7

Focus on Outcomes

At the highest level, organizations exist to reach outcomes of one sort or another. While it is in vogue for many of these "mission statements" to be a bit esoteric and written in corporatese, some of our favorites are more straightforward and make the point here much better:

> McDonald's: *McDonald's brand mission is to be our customers' favorite place and way to eat and drink.*[2]

> Google: *Google's mission is to organize the world's information and make it universally accessible and useful.*[3]

Of course, we have more than high-level goals. There are all types of goals, objectives, and targets. Sales teams have a quota and product mix that is clearly defined; projects have well-defined metrics for success, including time, budget, and standards.

While some might consider this a management conversation, we disagree. Reaching outcomes is clearly in the overlap between the management and leadership roles. Yes, you must manage the details of the metrics, but you must also attend to the underlying behaviors involved in reaching them.

If we don't focus on outcomes as a leader, we aren't doing what we were hired to do.

The Long-Distance Difference in Outcomes

As a Long-Distance Leader, this focus on outcomes is, if possible, even more important and can definitely be harder. We say that for several reasons:

- *Isolation.* When people are working remotely, they are likely alone more of the time. (Even if they are on a small team together but remote from you, what follows is still true.) Where we work forms a bubble around our habits, our thoughts, and the things we focus on. This isolation often leads to silos of the smallest nature—people acting as if they are a team of one, a Lone Ranger solving problems and making things happen from their home office desk. Over time, without guidance, they become focused on individual goals and key performance indicators (KPIs) rather than team goals. Leaders want a proactive, driven person working for them (wherever their desk is) but need to help them see how their outcomes are a part of the larger whole. Our jobs in communicating and clarifying goals can be harder at a distance.

- *Lack of environmental cues.* When you visit many organizational facilities, you will get a variety of messages about goals and priorities. Whether they're using a slogan like "Quality Comes First," a reader-board with the latest safety statistics, or a list of the corporate goals in every conference room, a common work location provides very clear clues and cues that reinforce important messages that are missing when you work from a home office.

- *(Potentially) less repetition of messages.* Unless leaders are consistently, and in a variety of ways, communicating and reiterating the goals and outcomes for the team and organization, people may get lost in their own bubble. This is particularly true if you have a matrixed team, where you are the nominal official leader yet the individuals report to others. Part of your role as a Long-Distance Leader is to find as many ways to keep people focused on the outcomes as possible. We can and should use online portals and other fancy tech tools to do this, but we need to do whatever it takes—personal notes, a whisper in the ear, or carrier pigeons even. You must communicate as often and as creatively as possible to keep all team members on board, in sync, and focused on the goals and objectives of team and the organization.

Focus on Others

As a leader, you have a myriad of things that vie for your attention:

- Budgets
- Projects
- Process improvements
- New product/service development
- Sales
- Customer service
- Margins

We bet at least part of this list resonates with you, and you could add a bunch more to it. You're thinking about all these things, and yet you aren't the one actually doing most of them.

So how do you overcome the conundrum of lots of important things and not knowing what to focus on?

You focus on something different than anything on the list above: *you put your focus on others.*

Figure 8

For example, you focus on the important things we purposely omitted from the earlier list, including:

- Coaching your team
- Communicating about priorities and projects
- Hiring
- Onboarding new team members
- Providing support and guidance

Long-Distance Leaders focus on others. Here are seven reasons why:

1. *You can't do it alone anyway.* Let's start with the most obvious of all— even if you tried, you couldn't do everything that needs doing all by yourself. And if you could, you wouldn't need a team, so there would be no need to be a leader. Leadership is about the outcomes, but those must be reached through others.

2. *You win when they win.* If you're going to focus on others, you must fundamentally believe this. You must believe that when you serve others, your needs will be met, your goals will be reached, and you will be recognized appropriately. True and lasting victory comes from helping others win too.

3. *You build trust when you focus on others.* Trust is a powerful lever for team and organization success. When trust is high, job satisfaction, productivity, and much more is improved. If you want to build trust with others, focus on them and show you trust them first.

4. *You build relationships when you focus on others.* There is a direct correlation between the strength of a relationship and the amount of trust that exists in that relationship. As trust increases, so does the strength of the relationship. Solid working relationships create better results. How do you build a relationship? You're interested in, listen to, and care about others.

5. *You are more influential when you focus on others.* As leaders, we can't force or compel people to take any action, or if we can it is for a limited time

and there will likely be other unforeseen consequences. We can't control people; we can only influence them. Think about it: Who is most successful in influencing you? Someone who you know understands your needs and situation. Someone who wants the best for you. Someone who is on your side of the table. So how can *you* do those things unless you are focused on others? Remember, influence is about helping others choose—you want more than mere compliance, don't you?

6. *Team members are more engaged when you focus on them.* This is profoundly true. People want to work with and for people who they know believe and care about them and have their best interests at heart.

7. *You succeed at everything on "the list" when you focus on others.* Look back at the list of things you "need to focus on" that we mentioned above. If you intentionally and purposefully focus on those around you, will those things all go better? While we're not saying you should ignore or completely delegate those things, we are saying is that if you focus on others first, the rest will be more successful more of the time.

We could make a longer list of reasons why placing your focus on others is the right choice, but anyone of the above is reason enough. Your role as a leader is to aid, support, guide, and help others reach valuable goals and outcomes. When you remember that and focus on them and their needs, you get better results for the organization, the team, and yes, yourself.

The long-distance difference for others

For reasons discussed throughout this book, maintaining this focus is harder at a distance. Here are some of the reasons why:

Out of sight can be out of mind. Kevin has a tangible example here. Several years ago, Marisa joined our team and worked in an office down the hall from Kevin. This was the context of the working relationship between them, until she got married (to Kevin's son, but we digress) and moved to South Bend, Indiana—about two and half hours away. She worked remotely nearly every day (she came to the Remarkable House—our office in Indianapolis—about once a month to do certain parts of her job). We held everything else static except her work location, and for Kevin to be equally as effective at helping Marisa succeed, giving her the resources, time, and encouragement she needed, he had to be far more diligent, creative, and disciplined while she was working remotely. The job got done; it just took a little more effort.

Happily, about eight months later, her husband (Kevin's son, stay with us) got a new job in Indianapolis, and now she is back in the office again. Marisa was doing a great job, regardless of her location. Kevin helped her achieve her goals by clearly defining what had to be done, checking in regularly, and leveraging webcams and other tools, and she stepped up and became much more independent and self-reliant. That said, is it easier for Kevin to be focused on Marisa's needs and be able to support and coach her from down the hall? Absolutely!

Your assumptions win the battle. As a leader, you make assumptions about your people, consciously or not. If you assume they are doing well, you will "worry" less about them. While this is true regardless of where people work, when you assume all is well and you don't see them, you don't communicate with them (as often). Or if you assume they'll let you know when they need help or support, or that no news is good news, or if you worry they will think you are "checking up" on them if you just want to check in, they may (and likely will) take your lack of communication/attention as a lack of focus on them—whether you mean for it to or not. Long-Distance Leaders must understand that scheduling when and how communication occurs is a conscious decision.

Even if you focus on them, do they know? The battle between perception and reality will always be won by perception. If your team members don't see the actions that show that you are thinking about them, want them to succeed, trust them, and more, it really doesn't matter what you are thinking or what your intention is. Kevin has long said "people watch our feet more than our lips," but when they are remote, they can't even watch our feet very easily. If you are to be truly Other focused, you must diligently show it to others through your actions.

Figure 9

Focus on Ourselves

The great paradox of leadership is that it isn't about us at all—as we have just said, fundamentally leadership is about outcomes and other people.

And yet, who you are, what you believe, and how you behave plays a huge role in how effectively you will do the other things. This is where Connie, most of the leaders in our survey, and likely you are encountering the most difficulty.

While this O is arguably the smallest of the three O's, it also in some ways must come first, even though as the model shows us, we must be last. Or, as we stated above, you are at the core of leadership, but certainly not at the center of your leadership universe.

The great paradox of leadership is that it isn't about us at all— fundamentally, leadership is about outcomes and other people.

You might know NFL star Gale Sayers' autobiography *I Am Third*. (If you ever saw the inspirational movie *Brian's Song*, this book was the impetus for that movie. If you haven't seen it, it is highly recommended. Bring plenty of tissues.) The title came from a line from his friend Brian Piccolo: "God is first, my family is second, and I am third." While our context here is different, the point is similar. While *who* you are and how you lead (Ourselves) can't be denied or ignored, if you think about Ourselves as third, you will serve both others and outcomes best.

While you may intellectually agree with what you just read, we need to say a bit more. Some would say it is about "how we show up in the world" and that since leaders can be successful in different ways, you should lead as who you are. This is true, but only to a point.

You can all bring who you are to your leadership, and there are many styles that can be successful in leading. And we do believe you need to be authentically you, but that isn't an excuse to stay where you are without choosing to change some of your behavior, constantly assess your priorities, build your skills, and get better!

At the core of you as a leader are the things you believe in and think about. Those drive your actions, how you engage with your team, how well you influence them, and ultimately how they will respond to and perform with you as their leader.

This book talks a lot about what you can do, and perhaps that is why you bought a copy. Ultimately what you want matters, and it's important only in the context of the other two O's—Outcomes and Others.

The long-distance difference for ourselves

Who you are and how you lead is important wherever your people work, but when you are leading at a distance, some of this is less transparent, and your beliefs and assumptions are even more crucial. Here are three reasons why:

Assumptions (again). You have assumptions about what it means to work remotely. We could give you the statistics that show teleworkers are more productive,[4] but if you don't believe that, or assume people are multitasking on non-work items while they are at work, you will operate based on that belief rather than the facts. Your assumptions about your team members always impact how you lead. When your folks are working at a distance, there is a very remote chance (pardon the pun) that your assumptions will ever be challenged—simply because you don't see enough evidence to change your mind. You also make assumptions about how much to ask of your people, and how much you're willing to adjust for things like time zones and meeting times. That's where Connie got in trouble—she assumed she solved the problem by working more. You must identify your assumptions about both yourself and those you lead, challenge them, and revise them when facts dictate.

Intention is important, but not enough. Throughout this book we talk about being intentional with nearly everything. Here, though, the challenge lies in the gap between what you want and mean to do, and what you actually do. Research shows that as humans we aren't very good at self-assessment in part because of this gap—we grade ourselves on what we are capable of or mean to do, while others view us based on our actions.[5] As you lead a team remotely, with less frequent interaction, and when much of that interaction is less rich and robust, it is much more likely that your team members won't see your intention, or will assume the worst, when you aren't quite meeting their needs. They don't know how swamped you are, or that you are stuck in the Des Moines airport; they just know you blew off their one-on-one.

Making a decision. This book will give you lots of ideas to apply—many of them could make a big difference in your ability to lead successfully. None of them will work until you decide to act. As a Long-Distance Leader, you must decide to do the unnatural things, you must focus (even) more on your team members, you must be diligent in supporting them and their needs, but you can't do those things until you decide that you are going to.

Connecting This to Other Models

We will be the first to admit that there are lots of models of leadership—in fact, elsewhere in this book we referenced Kevin's thirteen competencies of Remarkable Leadership—and all the best models provide a viewpoint into what it means to lead and how to do it well. Humbly, we submit that this Three O Model can sit on top of any of them (or on top of your organization's competency model) to provide an important perspective to them.

Regardless of the skills or competencies, in the end the best leaders will be effectively managing their focus and activity among their three O's, which are the things that everything about leadership rests on. This overview sets the table for the rest of this book. There is an entire section for each of the O's that will dive deeper and give you specific and concrete ways you can more effectively lead at a distance through the lens of each O.

Pause and Reflect

▶ What do you feel are the most important outcomes expected of you as a leader?

▶ How has working remotely impacted those outcomes for you and your people?

▶ What do you feel are the most important ways to focus on others in your organization?

▶ How has working remotely impacted that focus?

▶ How do you see yourself in your role as a leader?

▶ How has leading remotely impacted your beliefs and behaviors?

Section Three

Achieving Outcomes at a Distance

Section Three Introduction

Never mistake activity for achievement.

—John Wooden, Hall of Fame basketball coach

Raul is a new supervisor on a team of software engineers. He works from home and has for years, as has most of his team. His manager, though, has always worked out of the office and is very worried that team members might not be working as hard as they can. He's constantly asked, "How do you know what they're working on?" or "Are you absolutely positive we'll meet those deadlines?" Although in his gut he trusts his people, he struggles to assure his boss that real work is getting done, even when he can't peer over the cubicle and watch it.

As a leader, you're in the business of reaching desirable outcomes. Helping a team reach outcomes at a distance is a bit different, and so let's start there.

Here are some of the common questions we hear from survey respondents, whether they are new to the role or just struggling to get the job done:

- What are they doing?
- Are they accomplishing anything?
- Are they distracted working from home or wherever they are working?
- Are they working too much?

Let's come off the ledge, take a deep breath, and look at each of those questions.

What Are They Doing?

Though you can't see the people working remotely, how can you know what the people working down the hall are doing either? Are you looking over their shoulder all day? (If you are, perhaps you should start reading this book from the beginning again.) The specific answer here is hard to provide without knowing your industry and the work your folks do, but really, how is this any different whether they are in the next office or in the next state? Kevin was talking about this question with a client who agreed with him. She mentioned that she used to know someone who came to the office every day and basically clipped coupons all day. They looked busy; but clearly, they weren't getting any (work) outcomes! And they were in the office. You can't blame it on being remote.

Are They Accomplishing Anything?

You should have answers to this as a part of the work process and your role as leader and manager, right? And this should have nothing to do with where they are working. If you are thinking about this one, you are really thinking about the next question . . . .

Are They Distracted?

The fact is, they are likely less distracted than you or their down-the-hall team members are. Studies from *Harvard Business Review* and others show that people who work away from the office actually get more done on a task-by-task basis.[1] Some of that is for good reasons (lack of interruptions) and some for not-so-good reasons (they work more cumulative hours).

Even if you don't agree, let's just think about your personal experience. How many distractions and interruptions do you have during a workday in the office? And how many of them are caused by other people in that workplace with you? The distractions and productivity busters that are non-people related are likely the same for you and your remote folks, but they likely have far fewer people interruptions than you do. While there may be a person on your team who has trouble working remotely (and that is a coaching opportunity, not an indictment of everyone working remotely), the research shows that productivity will be higher for most people most of the time.

Are They Working Too Much?

That might not be the question you are asking, but you should. When people work remotely (especially from home), boundaries are harder to set. With our phones and devices always within reach, it is easy to check email in the evening (Josiah in Jordan could use this, I'll just respond now) or first thing in the morning; you get the idea. In fact, it's frequently a bit of a vicious cycle: Mary wants to look like she's working so she answers email as soon as she gets up in the morning and does it again after the kids are in bed. No wonder she's getting more done—she's putting in more hours. Is that what you really want?

Understanding whether people really are working harder or longer, or just time shifting some activities, is important, especially if you have a hybrid team, with some in the office and some working from home. Perception could be a significant problem: If Gina, who works in the office sees George sending emails at all hours, she may decide she needs to stay later or take her laptop home. Conversely, if George is working from home at 8:00 p.m., but the people in the office stop answering emails at five o'clock, he might wonder why they are all slackers.

We'll talk more about managing ourselves in section 5, but make sure you are setting reasonable expectations and boundaries for the team around expected response times, working hours, and working on the weekend.

The Real Issues

If these questions (or ones like them) bother you, there are likely three reasons:

- *You are focused on activity, not accomplishment.* Think about this question: Which is more important, how long or hard people work, or that the work is done correctly and on time? After all, it's the results (outcomes) we want, right? The questions above are focused on what or how people are doing work, not if they are getting quality work done. This may be a big focus change for you, and even if you agree intellectually, you might have trouble with this in practice. Kevin, though teaching and believing strongly in staying focused on results, has fallen victim to this thinking often. While he has rarely had standard working hours for team members, he's a morning person. It sometimes bothers him when someone comes to work (or logs in) later than he would. Then he remembers this important distinction and recognizes that if the quality of the work is the issue, why should he worry about it? Since it doesn't matter if that copy gets written at 9:00 a.m. or 6:00 p.m. as long as it's done by Friday's meeting, why does he concern himself with it? Getting clear about this is important: your job is to support people in getting the right work done in a quality way in the prescribed timelines. And let's address the elephant in the room: Why should it matter if they are doing their laundry during the workday, as long as the work is getting done and the rest of the team doesn't suffer as a result?

- *You think you would be distracted so you are projecting that on others.* You may be someone who struggles in the quiet environment of working from home or who needs the structure of getting in the car and going to the office. If so, that is fine (and yes, routines can be built to overcome some of those challenges if needed), but that doesn't mean everyone struggles with them just because you do, or you did once.

- *You fundamentally believe that "when the cat's away, the mice will play."* If you believe that people only work effectively when supervised, you are going to be hampered in leading any team, especially one that is remote. Do you think that just because you aren't there they are screwing off? Remember: If they are getting the work done, what are you really worrying about?

    Oh, and there is one more really important one too:

- *You have a perceived need for greater control.* Underlying at least some of the issues above is this fundamental point: if you are worried about your ability to lead remote team members to successful outcomes, you might have control issues. If people have been well trained, have the tools and resources they need, and have your support, they will be successful. If you struggle with control and tend to micromanage (and if you get that feedback consistently, you *are* micromanaging even if you don't think you are), you will be more challenged with leading remotely.

    If you were nodding your head at any of these items you just read, we have some suggestions for you.

Build processes together. Job aids, procedures, checklists, and proven templates to help people do the work are key to good performance and critical in a remote environment, where people can't easily watch and learn from their peers. When people have input into what those processes are, the engagement and success will be even higher and compliance more likely. And, these processes may provide a clue to people's progress and status; in other words, they may be a predictive measure of progress and accomplishment.

Create mutually clear expectations. It is important to define and agree on the expectations of the work and the results—and how you'll measure success. When people know their peers are committed to responding before the end of the day, there's less sitting around fuming when they don't get an immediate response. Also, when people are part of creating the rules, they take responsibility for abiding by them and being better teammates. This is especially important for project teams, where people depend on input from each other on a regular basis. But even on sales teams, where it often feels like "every person for themselves," it helps keep everyone connected and reduces the perception of favoritism.

Change your belief. Listen to the research, pay more attention, and you will likely change your perspective on the productivity of people who aren't working in the office. They will likely be very productive, especially if you have taken our advice.

Reduce your need for control. We know that may be easier to say than do, but we encourage you to think about what you can influence rather than what you can control. Make sure people have the skills and training they need, provide them feedback and encouragement, give them resources and tools to be successful, and then *let them do it*. And beyond those actions, repeat after us: let it go.

Chapter 6

Types of Outcomes

Rule 6: Leading successfully requires achieving goals of many types.

People with goals succeed because they know where they are going.
—Earl Nightingale, writer and radio host

Angela leads a team of customer service reps working from home. Each of those people has individual goals—the number of calls a day, how many are handled on the first call, how many get escalated to a manager, among others. The reps are also encouraged to share experiences and best practices and let each other know where to find the information they need in a hurry. Angela has noticed that the individual metrics are being met, but few people are using the shared file sites or answering each other's questions. So, while some of the goals are clearly met, the overall team communication isn't what it should be. When everyone worked in the call center she didn't have this problem, and she's not sure what to do about it now.

It is one thing to say (or write) "leadership is about outcomes," but that's neither specific nor helpful. After all, there are lots of different outcomes you are trying to reach in an organization. As a Long-Distance Leader, you need to be aware of, think about, and help your teams reach all of them.

As you read through the rest of this chapter, don't just nod in agreement with the descriptions—read what follows like a checklist. Ask yourself how much you focus in this area and how often your conversations with your team members touch on each of these types of outcomes.

Organizational Outcomes

There are reasons your organization exists, and if you, your team, and the organization collectively aren't tending to those reasons well enough, it might not be a good outcome! Depending on the size of your organization, you might be involved in setting these organizational targets, or you might only be responsible for understanding and helping your team reach the targets set for them.

For example, if you work in a smaller organization, you might be in the meeting where the organizational goals for the year are set. If so, your level of understanding (and hopefully commitment) to those goals should be strong. If you are a middle manager in a Fortune 500 company, you likely weren't at the retreat where they were set, but your need to understand and be able to communicate them successfully is no less important.

Regardless of how the targets are set and who sets them, as a leader they must be crystal clear so you can help your team members (individually and collectively) move toward successfully achieving them. The bigger your organization, the more levels might exist (e.g., division, business unit) between you and the full organizational targets. It's your responsibility to understand, communicate, and align the work of your team with these targets, however many levels of them there might be. Consider these questions:

- How clear are these targets?

- How often do you think about them?

- How often does your team discuss or review these targets to track progress?

Team Outcomes

There are larger organizational targets, some of which paint the big picture but might seem a bit esoteric to your team. Team targets are the specific outcomes your team is responsible for achieving. While your role in creating organizational targets will vary with the size of your organization and your culture, at the team level this responsibility rests squarely on you. We've worked with leaders in nearly every type of organization, and far too often team targets are weak. We find the reasons include:

- *They are assumed*—"Everybody knows what our goals are."

- *They are too vague*—"Get the product out the door" isn't really a goal.

- *They are under-reviewed*—"We talked about those last December at the annual meeting."

When your team is in the same location, you catch side conversations and parking lot banter and have many ways to reinforce and clarify the goals. When you have team members working on their own, these clarifications don't happen easily. People must know how what they do fits into the work and success of the team. Ask yourself these questions:

- How clear are your team targets?

- How much time are you thinking about them?

- Do all your team members know these targets?

- Are there signs there might be confusion over those goals?

- How often are you reviewing progress?

Personal/Individual Outcomes

People need to know what outcomes they're responsible for, what targets they are shooting for, and what qualifies as success. Even when people are integral parts of a team effort, individual targets are needed. Think about this from a sports perspective. The team has an organizational outcome in mind (winning a championship), team results (wins and losses), and perhaps results for a portion of the team (offense, defense, or some subset of the larger team). And yet even with all those outcomes, individual players need targets too (personal objectives measured by individual performance or statistics). Beyond the short-term targets, they must be thinking beyond their role to their overall career development—and as leaders we have a role to play there too.

Leaders must be concerned with both team and individual results. Too often individual goals become the sole focus for the remote team member. Collaboration is harder when you're working remotely; it simply doesn't happen as easily or organically. Leaders need to be aware of this and help facilitate this communication.

Remember that working remotely can be like living alone on an island. There is less interaction, and none of it happens serendipitously. Without solid, clear targets, individuals can drift, losing sight of both the big picture and their role too. That's why tools like electronic dashboards, intranets, and online project management systems are so important—they provide visibility even when people are miles apart.

One more thing here: team members who are "on their island" may be less aware of the individual contributions, roles, and goals of their teammates (who are in the office, on their own islands, or both). When people don't have any clue about the work of others, they are less likely to understand the questions they get from them, assume they aren't busy or their work isn't important, and much more. This lack of awareness and understanding can cause team rifts, poor communication, frustration, and conflict. As a leader, it is your responsibility to ensure people hear about the good work of their peers and get a chance to build trust in each other. It doesn't matter if you are busy or if it is hard to do—this is one of the remote leadership challenges you must accept.

As a Long-Distance Leader, make sure that your remote team members have context for the roles and targets of other team members too. You also need to decide how often you'll check in with each team member on these metrics. This will help keep your remote team members from feeling either abandoned or micromanaged.

But Wait, There's More

We've just described the core list of the outcomes that any leader in any type of organization must be aware of. We've also talked about the results that need to be achieved. But there is a more granular and more operational type of outcome we haven't even mentioned yet.

When you think about outcomes, you likely think about results, and you would probably call what we have just described as goals. The importance of goals can't be overstated, and we are going to talk about how to set them with a remote team in the next section. But these results goals are only one type of outcome we need to discuss here. On a daily working basis, perhaps more important than goals are expectations.

Expectations aren't just about the "big G" goals or the "what needs to happen." They are about how the work gets done: the rules for working together, the way you'll support and help each other, what tools you'll use, and what good communication looks like.

Clear, mutually understood and agreed-to expectations are the necessary foundation for successful performance—and a more successful (calmer and less stressed) you. In other words, when the expectations are clear and understood, the chances people will be successful are higher. Furthermore, there's a better chance the outcomes described above will be reached.

When Kevin starts workshops, he usually does an exercise to get people to clarify their goals and expectations for the learning experience. It involves writing down and sharing those ideas with others. In the debrief that follows, the group identifies some important points about expectations that directly apply to their work:

- *Expectations provide clarity.* They become clearer when they are written down. Are the expectations you have of your team members written down, or are they assumed?

- *Expectations provide focus and set priorities.* They help people be clear on what is most important among the list. Do you have folks who have a mismatch with you on the most important or relevant parts of the work?

- *Expectations provide context.* Sharing the expectations verbally helps everyone understand both their own and the expectations of the others in the group. This helps eliminate silos within your team. Have you talked with your people about their expectations?

- *Expectations must be mutually and explicitly agreed to.* Unless there is explicit agreement, people are left to make their own assumptions, and the less frequently they interact, the more likely there's a disparity in expectations. Remember that simply sending an email without discussion doesn't create true clarity or agreement.

How can your team members meet your expectations if they don't know what they are?

Before you think everyone on your team "has to know" your expectations of them, let us ask you another question.

As you read this, are you thinking about a member of your team who you really want to "fix"? Have you been reading in part to see how you could lead that one person more effectively?

If so, ask yourself this question: Do they know what you expect of them? Because just like Kevin's workshop situation, if they don't know what you expect, how can they possibly deliver?

Setting clear, mutually understood expectations with team members is one of the most important things you can do as a leader. In doing so, you are doing the simplest thing you can to improve the chances that people will achieve the desired outcomes for their role. The importance of doing this for the success and confidence of the other person, and *your* sanity, can hardly be overstated.

It may seem that doing this remotely may be even more important (if that is possible) because your team members are out on their own with less interaction with you to help guide and set expectations. In our experience, though, many leaders aren't doing this very well with their team members down the hall either. Invest the time in your team members to help this become clear to them, regardless of work location, and you will give them a much clearer picture of the outcomes that will make them successful.

Pause and Reflect

- ▶ Are your organizational outcomes clear?

- ▶ Are your team outcomes clear?

- ▶ Are the individual outcomes with each team member clear?

- ▶ Are expectations within your team clear?

- ▶ If not, when will you start making all of this clear?

Online Resources

For more resources to go:

www.LongDistanceLeaderBook.com/Resources

To assess how clear and aligned your team is on goals, register at the website below and request the **Team Goal Clarity Tool**.

To build more effective remote work routines when people don't go to an office, request the **Building Remote Work Routines Checklist**.

Chapter 7

Setting (and Achieving) Goals at a Distance

Rule 7: Focus on achieving goals, not just setting them.

Setting a goal is not the main thing. It is deciding how you will go about achieving it and staying with that plan.

—Tom Landry, Hall of Fame football coach

Frank has been a sales manager for five years. He's always had a couple of people who work from home offices, but most of his people have worked together except when they're out with customers. Over the last year, his people have been working from home more and coming into the office less frequently. His top performers are still making quota, and many are outdistancing their goals, but he's noticed that newer hires are struggling. He's spending more time with them, and they aren't getting the benefit of the old-timers' war stories and advice. The team's total number still looks good, but he's spending way too much time managing individual salespeople and not enough working on strategic planning. He's spending more time on goals he used to be able to "set and forget."

In our opinion, there is a major gap in the literature around goal setting. Pick up any book about the subject (you know, the one gathering dust on your shelf) and you will find it does a fine job of outlining a very specific process for setting goals. This usually isn't the problem. The problem is that most books don't focus on how to achieve the goals you painstakingly set.

This plays out in organizations and on teams everywhere. The organization has a deadline for when annual goals will be set. Work and focus are placed on this goal-setting process, with meetings slipped into time blocks where the "real" work is normally being accomplished. The goals are finalized and submitted, and the group (and/or leader) breathe a collective sigh. There is a celebration of sorts, or at least an acknowledgment of the task before everyone returns to work. Then, about nine or ten months later, the process is repeated.

The problem organizations face mirror our problem with all those books: the focus is all on *setting* the goals, when it should be on achieving the goals.

The problem organizations face mirror our problem with all those books: the focus is all on *setting* the goals, when it should be on achieving the goals.

If you identify in any way with the somewhat cynical scenario we just described, we have good news: you can change that—and when you make this change, your team will quickly get better and have more lasting results.

Now that we have shared our perspective here, let's talk a bit about setting more effective goals in a remote environment and spend some important time on how we can help those goals get achieved.

Setting Goals Remotely

Most everyone agrees that goals should be SMART, a clever mnemonic that authors like to use. While not everyone uses the same words to complete the memory device, here is what we use:

- Specific
- Measurable

- Actionable

- Realistic

- Time-driven

The reason the mnemonic has become ubiquitous is that it is hard to argue with the wisdom of the five attributes. When those attributes are true about a goal statement, you have improved the chances that the goal will be reached.

In our experience, people find two of these criteria the hardest to master and the most difficult to make work from a distance: making goals measurable, and determining what realistic looks like. Let's talk about each and identify the nuances of these challenges when you are not right there.

Making Goals Measurable

Some goals are easy to measure. If you are leading salespeople (remotely or otherwise), you don't have any issues here; after all, a sales goal is clearly measurable. Look at the sales numbers and you will know where you are and how close you are to the goal. There are many other roles where you don't have to think too hard to find measurable targets. With other jobs, there may not be an obvious financial or tangible target, and you might have to work harder to create measurable goals.

To make the work of others more measurable, ask how else you can quantify the effort and contributions of others. These questions might help:

- What are the *quantity* components of the work?

- How does *time* factor into the success of the work?

- How is the *quality* of the work determined?

Remember, although we have tried to dispel the worries you might have about what people are doing when you can't see them working every day, when you can find measurable targets your concerns in this area should be reduced. While measurements should always be clear, when working with team members who are remote, setting measures in smaller chunks can be even more important. When people work alone, in their own bubble, and the targets are too big, it is easy to let too much time pass before realizing the need to course correct. Maybe they're struggling with a challenge but don't want to admit

75

they're having trouble. Or perhaps they are working under assumptions that are no longer true because they literally missed the memo.

Wayne calls these Wile E. Coyote moments. In the classic Road Runner cartoons, Wile E. Coyote is often in such hot pursuit of his target (the Road Runner) that he runs off the edge of the cliff. We laugh in the pause before he falls to the canyon floor, but it isn't a laughing matter to him. Nor will it be to your team members when they realize they've gone too far and need to start over, do a bunch of rework, or make major adjustments. Measuring progress frequently, and with intent, makes a difference. If you can see that Margaret is on track with her work, you can relax. If you know that Bob is nearing deadline, you might want to check in to see if he needs additional resources or help with anything.

While these questions certainly help, they don't solve the challenge of making goals measurable for all jobs or all parts of every job.

Think about Frank our sales manager. Certainly he's measuring how many outbound calls or appointments his reps do. But is he checking on how often they've talked to their peers? If sharing of best practices is a goal at the team level, has his top producer contributed to the Q & A site or helped a newbie as Frank has asked him to?

Two Types of Goals

We've already talked about the *what* and the *how* of people's work. Most people think about goals in terms of "what" (or results) goals, which we have just discussed. But that doesn't always cut it, or it doesn't give a full picture of *how* people are doing (or "process" goals). If you are still a bit worried about how to know what your folks are doing when they aren't working in the office, these types of goals can help you tremendously.

The Jerry Seinfeld Strategy?

Search the internet and you will find a goal-achievement strategy attributed to Jerry Seinfeld.[1] The concept is sound and why we share it here.

The idea is simple: if the results goal is being a better comic, the process goal might be writing new jokes every day. Jerry encouraged a young comedian to get a big full-year calendar and place it on a wall where she could see it.

Then, he told her to put an X with a red marker on each day that she wrote new jokes. The goal then is to keep the chain of X's intact.

We can attest that this strategy works, and once you think about it, you can see it in many places:

- There are a bevy of "habit apps" such as Lifehacker and Productive that fundamentally provide this calendar.[2]

- This type of activity measure is a key tool in gamification, i.e., making activities and learning more like a game.

- The correlation between this strategy and addiction-cessation groups (Alcoholics Anonymous, Narcotics Anonymous, etc.) is clear.

Maybe the X is on an online dashboard (tools like SharePoint, your intranet, or your project management software), where you and your remote team members can easily access and see it. Maybe progress is reported weekly, to both the employee and the leader, or maybe you discuss them in your ongoing one-on-ones (more on these later). Use your circumstances, the nature of the work, and the members themselves to determine how you do it (which could be measured as a process goal). When you figure that out, you have more measurable goals.

What about Realistic?

The other question we hear about SMART goals is, "How do you know it is realistic?" Here is what that *shouldn't* mean:

- It isn't a slam dunk that it will be reached.

- It isn't so big that people don't really believe it is possible.

A realistic goal is one that stretches your belief, yet you can create a workable real-world plan that might allow you to reach that goal.

Think of a rubber band and the tension it can provide. If we let the rubber band lay limp on the desk, it doesn't help us in any way. When we pull it past its breaking point, it is of no value to us either. This is analogous to the slam-dunk goal—it's like the target that is so big that it doesn't help us, and in fact de-motivates us. But when we stretch the rubber band just enough, the tension begs us to move in the direction of the tension. This is our metaphor for a powerful and helpful realistic target, and why setting them at the right level is so important.

Like Goldilocks and the porridge, too cold and too hot aren't great; you want it just right.

We wish we could give you a specific and solid definition or answer to the "what is realistic anyway" or "what is just right" questions, but like all good consultants, we'll start by saying "it depends."

What does "realistic" depend on?

- *Past performance.* If last year your team member completed four process improvement projects, five or six might be realistic but ten might not be. If you have a team member who did nine last year, ten seems like a slam dunk, and maybe thirteen or fourteen is a better target.

- *Level of confidence.* Confidence plays a role in achievement. If you have a team member who's confidence in general, or just on this task, is low, you will want to take that into account when setting a realistic goal. This isn't an excuse for low performance, but it is part of your role as a leader to help them build their confidence so that they can achieve at higher levels.

- *Recent development or skill trajectory.* How are people building their skills? If they have done far better in the last quarter than the previous three, perhaps the annual goal is based on the more recent performance, not the full year.

- *Outlook on the world.* Related to confidence, the cynics or Eeyores of the world will feel like the goals need to be lower too—they see the obstacles, pitfalls, and potential negatives easily. This is a coaching opportunity, yet you must remember that people's personal beliefs will impact what they see as realistic.

Making Them Realistic

Here are some suggestions to make the goals of your remote team members more realistic. (This is a good overall process for setting them collaboratively too—it just happens to help create realistic targets at the same time.)

1. *Provide the needed information.* Make sure everyone knows what this year's performance is, what the organizational targets for next year are, and the relative importance and priority of the goal being set.

2. *Expect engagement.* Let people know (especially if this is a new idea for them) that the goal-setting process will be collaborative. Ask them to come to the discussion prepared, and expect that preparation to be more than a thought as they turn on their webcam. Without the visual information, you can't see the worried look on their face or their shoulders slump in despair. Remember, there's a big difference between compliance and buy-in.

3. *Get their thoughts first.* If you want realistic goals that people will be committed to, you must create a conversation. As the boss, you won't have a conversation if you start talking first or if you dominate the conversation. If they aren't prepared with their thoughts about the goals, it's better to reiterate the needs and your desire for them to be prepared (and reschedule) rather than plowing forward with your ideas first. Be careful that you set aside enough time for this, as it's more common to worry about "wasting time" in a virtual environment than it is when you're sitting together over a cup of coffee. Not only does this need to be a priority, the employee needs proof that it's important.

4. *Modify with your thoughts, if needed.* If you want them to have ownership of the goals, the goals need to be theirs. But if they set targets that you deem as too easy or not quite in alignment with the organizational needs, you may need to help them stretch the rubber band. Don't just unilaterally change the target—talk about it. Help them see that a bigger target can be realistic to both of you. Ensure that the conversation raises their comfort and confidence in reaching that raised target. Just because you want agreement doesn't mean you have to acquiesce to the target they pick—you are the leader, after all.

5. *Gain agreement.* Once you have SMART goals that everyone can live with, you have your best chance of hitting the goal. If you work toward

true agreement, you might only get to understanding or compliance. Even then, the conversation is worth the time.

So far we've been talking about individual goals, but the same rules apply to group objectives. Whether you have the whole team together for this conversation or you are using your web-conference tools, the process is the same. Kevin uses this basic approach in setting the company's revenue targets each year. If the goal is to have team ownership of the targets, it must begin with people having the information they need and creating a conversation about the targets. If Kevin provides the targets as the boss and then asks, "What do you think?" he'll likely get one of two responses:

- Disagreement, with no clear way to move forward.

- Acquiescence, where people will tacitly agree but never really have owner-ship of the target or much sense of how realistic it is. Again, compliance is not ownership, and when you're not in the room you miss a lot of the visual and nonverbal cues that will tell you which you're getting.

Making the goals or targets realistic is important, and you will know they are realistic when they provide guidance and motivation for those affected and are agreed to by you and the others involved.

Plan for Achievement Early

We've said that too often the focus (organizationally and personally) is on setting goals and not on achieving them. The easiest and most tangible way to overcome this common problem is linking the goal-setting and goal-planning processes together.

Energy, enthusiasm, and goal clarity are often highest when goals are first set. Take advantage of this by spending time on planning for goal achievement as soon as possible after setting the goals.

If you create the goals collaboratively, you might not want to go to planning immediately (but if you reach agreement quickly, you might have time to dive in), but close the meeting by deciding when you will finish the planning. Get it on the calendar and decide what technology to use for this important next step. As long as the plan is created within the next few days, you will capitalize on most of these "early mover" benefits.

Reaching Them Remotely

Even if you plan goal-achievement steps as quickly as you can after setting the goals, that isn't the full story. You must execute the plan and do the work to reach the goals. Here is the thing—if reaching goals were easy, there wouldn't be so many books written about it.

Goals aren't achieved in a vacuum. Priorities shift, emergencies arise, and stuff happens. When all of that occurs remotely, it is even harder to recognize, offer assistance, and change gears. Often employees make decisions on their own that impact their long-term goals and those of the team, and you won't know until it's too late. As a Long-Distance Leader, you and your people need to have a process that allows for the unexpected while keeping everyone on the same track.

Set clear expectations up front

Once you have a plan, make sure everyone is clear that the plan isn't a suggestion but a road map. Even a GPS recalculates as needed but keeps you headed toward your goal. Make sure both parties (you and the team member) understand the plan and have thought through how it will work in the realities of daily work and what to do when the unexpected arises.

Visualize them

In 1971 when Disney World opened, Roy Disney (Walt's brother and a company executive) was asked what Walt would have thought if he could see it completed (Walt died during construction). Roy's short answer: "You don't understand. Walt already saw it. That is why we are here." When we take time to help people literally see the result in three dimensions, the goal will more likely be reached. Tap into this 3-D picture in conversations with people, especially when the challenges mount and they are frustrated by a lack of progress. When this happens with remote team members, use your web-conferencing tools and webcams to make the conversations as effective as possible.

Expect consistent implementation

The best way to reach a goal is to be working on it regularly. Remember the Seinfeld "strategy"? Encourage your team members to consistently work on their goal achievement plan. Individual steps don't have to be big; it's progress that matters—regular small advances typically outpace the occasional big effort.

Make progress on goal plans a regular part of your conversations and one-on-ones. This communication keeps you in the loop, helps you remove barriers quickly, and reinforces the importance of reaching the goal. This will reduce stress on both parties—as the leader you are getting the information you need, but because it has been mutually agreed to, your team member likely won't see you as micromanaging them.

Provide time

If the goals are important enough to be set, time must be provided to work on them. As a leader you must help people manage their time and allow enough discretionary time for goal work to happen. Remember that when people work remotely, they may solve this problem by working more hours or unintentionally neglecting tasks that others rely on. Help them be successful by planning their time realistically.

Protect the time

Working on goals is important work. We'll bet you have scheduled important work on your calendar before but had it slip away when a meeting came up or the urgent items of the day melted that scheduled time away. While we wouldn't wish this on anyone, imagine this hypothetical for a second. If you had previously experienced some heart problems and you had a scheduled appointment with your cardiologist, would you cancel it for the same kinds of reasons you cancel other appointments with yourself? Probably not.

When you (or your team members) schedule time to work on something important—like goal achievement or an important project—allow that time to be sacred, like "cardiologist time." When your remote team members are comfortable enough to schedule time like that and have a way to communicate it with others so that they can be undisturbed, your whole team will achieve more goals faster than you imagined. For this to work best as a remote or hybrid team, calendars must be shared and there must be a forum for discussing deadlines and priorities.

Make it a priority

If the only time the goals are a priority is when you set them, you haven't much chance of achievement and perhaps would have been better off not to set them at all. If you are doing the other things on this list, the goals will be (and be seen as) a priority to your team members.

Report and discuss regularly

One of the best things you can do to help people achieve their goals is to talk about them regularly. This means real conversation, not just "reporting out." Progress reports or status updates are great, but they don't tell you if someone is concerned about something or is overly confident. Make progress on goals a part of your conversations if you want to achieve more. Setting smaller, incremental targets creates more reasons to connect more frequently. Remember, you won't bump into each other in the hallway, so you need be more intentional about these short but critical interactions.

Provide resources

Part of your job as leader is to help people remove the barriers and give them the tools and resources to make their plan happen. Time is one resource, but there may be others, like helping them know who else in the organization they can rely on for information or expertise. Do your job—help them reach the goals that have been set.

Be flexible

One of the biggest complaints we hear about goal setting in organizations is that the world is changing so fast that setting goals isn't productive—because things change too fast. There is truth here—mergers happen, new projects arrive, new products are developed, and priorities shift. You need to be flexible with the goals and their priority and be willing to move some to the back burner (or remove them from the list). Our advice here is twofold:

- Acknowledge that things might change as the year goes on.

- Work together to make the required adjustments.

Pause and Reflect

▶ Are your goals SMART?

▶ Have you considered process goals as well as results goals?

▶ Are you using enough of them?

▶ Are you placing too much focus on setting the goals . . . and in effect not spending enough focus on the plan for achieving them?

▶ How can you help your team reach the goals that have been set?

Online Resource

If you want to create team goals collaboratively at a distance, register at

LongDistanceLeaderBook.com/Resources

and request the **Remote Goal Setting Checklist.**

Chapter 8

Coaching and Feedback at a Distance

Rule 8: Coach your team effectively regardless of where they work.

One of the best things you can do for other people
is to help them recognize how they can improve.

—Wess Roberts, author

Helen is struggling with her customer service team. Half are in the call center, the rest work from home. She knows that coaching and ongoing feedback is critical to the success of her team, and she's always done a good job of coaching and developing them. Recent feedback, though, shows that the people she co-locates with are much happier with her coaching efforts than her remote folks. She's struggling to schedule time with those who work from home, and the coaching sessions are much less satisfying for both her and the employees. She's wondering what she is doing wrong and if it's even possible to be as effective at a distance as it is in the same location.

Coaching in general is a broad topic, and entire books and curricula are built around the subject. At the beginning of this book, we made some assumptions, one of which is that you already are familiar with most of the basics of leadership, which includes the need for and willingness to coach your people. If your organization has a prescribed model or process for coaching, what follows will augment those efforts well. If you don't already have a pre-scribed method for coaching, we suggest the simple model outlined in Kevin's book *Remarkable Leadership*.

The Remote Difference

If we were to pick a big area of leadership competence that needs improve-ment, it would be coaching. Coaching is also the area that Long-Distance Leaders routinely feel they could improve. Time seems scarce, conversations can be uncomfortable or seem more difficult at a distance, and leaders often don't feel confident that they're doing it well. Working remotely creates an additional layer of complexity to the part of the job in which we're already least secure. The fundamentals of coaching—having clear goals, building a relation-ship, providing both encouragement and correction—don't change whether you're in the same room or an ocean apart, but somehow it seems harder.

There are two big reasons coaching remotely feels more complicated and stressful:

Every interaction needs to be conscious and intentional. When you aren't working in the same location, you don't run into people in the break room or catch them out of the corner of your eye and wander over to their cubicle for a quick chat. You need to intentionally get their attention and take time out of whatever else you (and they) are working on. If you're the kind of person who's tempted to avoid these types of conversations anyway, working remotely makes it easier not to do what you need to do.

Communicating through technology creates mental and social obstacles that don't exist face-to-face in person. We naturally communicate best when we are physically in the presence of other people. When we are remote, we are working through technology that may feel like a barrier, and we feel pressed for time. If you've ever caught yourself beginning an online conversation with "this will only take a minute and then you can get back to work" and then rushed through what should have been a meatier discussion, you know what we mean.

What follows is true about all coaching, but it is designed to address these two issues that are particularly troubling when you're at a distance.

Keep accountability clear

Great coaches care and think about the performance and skills of their team members. As a leader, you feel responsible if someone doesn't perform well. You may think about what else you could have taught them, another way to have inspired them, or any number of other things. While it is important to think about what else you could have done, in the end, the final accountability for performance lies with the performer. Your job is to promote the confidence, skill, and proficiency of the other person, because they are doing the work.

Check your beliefs

Whatever you believe about your team member will drastically impact their ability to be successful in their work. Think about it this way: if you believe someone can be successful, you will be looking for the clues, examples, emails, and results that confirm your belief in them. But the opposite is also true. Once you have an opinion about someone, you've decided. And as true as that is when you work face-to-face with people every day, it is even more true when you don't see them as often.

This is called confirmation bias, which is enhanced in a remote environment because you have less data to draw on. People are usually less aware of conflicting evidence because they don't process electronic information the same way they do in person. Because you often scan emails, unless something really jumps out at you, you're likely to miss subtle clues that don't fit your notions of that person's competence and motives.

Assume positive intent; be prepared to be wrong

Consider the two basic assumptions we make about people's capabilities and the results they lead to:

- At the start of the coaching conversation you assume the best—that the person's intent was in the right place; that even if they messed up or fell short of a goal or deadline, there were plausible and understandable reasons, not including ineptitude.

- At the start of the coaching conversation you assume the worst—that the person was aware of the gap but apparently didn't care, or was in some way unaware of the problem.

Isn't it fair to say that your initial assumption will affect the way you ask questions and give feedback? We believe that starting from a place of positive intent will be more accurate more of the time and get better coaching results.

Wayne says that this is one of Kevin's great strengths, but like any strength it can become a weakness, which is why we added "be prepared to be wrong." You can assume positive intent and be wrong. And when you are, you need to coach from a more stern and clear position. These conversations may not be easy, especially remotely, but using the lessons we have shared throughout the book, we believe you can succeed.

Remember that coaching isn't about where people are today but where they can be. You must look for reasons to believe in others and their potential. If you don't start with the belief that people are coachable, you won't do it. If they are remote you might have to try harder. That's okay, because it is worth the effort.

Make sure it is truly a real conversation

Too many coaches do too much of the talking too much of the time. If you want to be a better coach, you must create a real two-way conversation with the other person about their behavior and results. The best way to do this is to ask them first, and create a conversation *with them speaking first*. When doing this remotely, make the conversation as effective as possible. (This is one time to make webcams your friend. More on this below.) When there is a pause in the conversation, end the silence with a question, not a statement.

It's easy to fall into the trap of doing too much of the talking, especially if you are on the phone and can't gauge how the other person is reacting. Remember that if you talk to end a silence, you are teaching others to be quiet and let you talk. If you are doing all the talking, their ownership is likely diminishing sentence by sentence. This is especially true because you are the boss ("the boss is talking, so I better let them talk"). The power structure is so weighted in your favor that you must do everything you can to strike a balance. Ask more first, and talk less.

Make sure the job expectations are crystal clear

As we saw in our Three O Model, first and foremost leaders must coach toward achieving outcomes. Just because expectations are clear doesn't mean they are all being met, yet effective coaching hinges on clear expectations. If people aren't clear on the expectations, this becomes job one in the coaching process and must happen before anything else takes place. One of the best ways to make them crystal clear is by putting them in writing. We believe that may actually be easier with a remote team member.

If you just use the phone, you may naturally wonder if the other person is writing things down or is even listening. When you are using technology to have the coaching conversation, the notes and documented expectations can be visible to both of you on the devices you are working on to facilitate the conversation. This makes for easier reference and clarity during and after the conversation. You should share a screen to enable creation of, or reference to, the document together. This increases the odds of gaining the needed clarity. You're literally seeing things the same way.

Have a process

As we have already said, if you have a coaching process, use it. Most coaching models are built assuming face-to-face communication, but if you stop and consider all the ideas in this book (including the chapters to come on communication and technology use), you'll be fine. While team members don't need to know the model or approach you are using, they'll benefit from the consistency that it creates in the way you coach. You reduce the angst and uncertainty others will have when they know more about how—and how often—you will coach.

Make coaching consistent and frequent

We can't say this enough: people need ongoing coaching and feedback. Think about it this way: if you do something well but never get any feedback, you might unknowingly change it and make it worse, or at a minimum keep trying new approaches with varying success. If you get some feedback that you are on the right track, you will lock in the behavior and start to create a habit.

Alternatively, if you are doing something wrong and not knowing, you may keep doing it assuming it is fine, and build a habit of doing it wrong. Both can be avoided by providing ongoing feedback. Have a recurring timeline for formal, scheduled coaching. When working remotely there will be a temptation to keep it short and infrequent. Don't surrender—this is critical time and should be a priority. There will also be informal coaching moments, which we'll talk about shortly.

Use your webcam

Coaching is important enough to make the communication as effective as possible. Why do we think face-to-face is better than using the phone? Because we rely on visual and nonverbal cues to help us communicate. Our brains crave visual connection to the people we speak with. Webcams, and other tools we'll discuss in the next section, help mitigate the fact that you're not in the same room.

We know that many people are uncomfortable being on camera, and if we're already reluctant to have tough conversations, doing it in a way that makes us squirm is not going to help. Comfort comes with repetition. The more people use them, the less stressed they will be. For reluctant web-camers, it is okay to not force their use all the time—they will appreciate that acknowledgment and flexibility. Just know that if you only ask them to use webcams for what you perceive as the tough conversations, you have a new problem of raising stress before the conversations even begin! Be flexible, but request/insist on using the cams some of the time so that using it doesn't always mean that this is a "big deal" conversation.

Follow up

Too often, there is a coaching conversation, a plan of action determined to help people move forward, and then . . . nothing. Whether follow-up doesn't happen because of a lack of discipline, poor time management, or assuming the best, your team members will treat the coaching or the gap in performance as if it wasn't *that* important. In the worst case, a cynical team member might not love the once-a-quarter conversation about their reports being late, but it is easier to endure an occasional conversation than change their behavior because without follow-up, *your* behavior tells them it *isn't* that important. As frequently as coaches of teams that are down the hall mess this up, remote leaders are often worse.

Sometimes, Helen, our customer service manager, would get off the phone and then remember she wanted to talk to Alice about something, but the opportunity has passed. Or the call happens while she's in transit and so needs to be as short as possible, which is not ideal for the kind of conversations we're talking about. At least when you're working together, you can see someone in the hallway or pass by their desk and that may prompt you to speak to that person. When people aren't seen, you can't rely on spontaneity; you must be focused and intentional about all your follow-up.

Check in, don't check up

We love the phrase "check in, don't check up," because even the most confident, skilled team members will be fine (and usually appreciate) when you check in with them on how things are going, especially if these check-ins are regular and expected. And even the least seasoned person who may not be performing very well at all doesn't like to be "checked up on." The difference between the two is often perception.

First, make sure that your intention is to support and help by checking in, not by figuratively looking over their shoulder. The best way to manage this perception is to plan in advance how you can help, as well as when and how you will be available, and hopefully gain agreement on how, and how often, you'll communicate when setting your goals and expectations. By reaching agreement on the frequency of these check-in points early, you improve the chances that your intention won't be misread.

You have to coach, even when it's uncomfortable

Coaching is part of a leader's job, but at a distance, it can be tempting to take the easy way out. You have a team member who is doing something poorly or making an error. Maybe it isn't a big problem, but it still needs to be addressed. You put it off and secretly hope it will get better, or you just don't like confrontation, so you send an email instead of having a conversation. Some leaders use time zones as the excuse for avoiding addressing a problem as proactively as they should. By ignoring, procrastinating, or avoiding the need for the coaching, you are giving tacit approval, and the behavior will continue. Why shouldn't it? Just because you don't see someone in the hallway several times a day doesn't mean you can take the easy way out and avoid providing the coaching they need so they can succeed.

Giving Feedback

Feedback isn't coaching, but almost all coaching includes feedback. Here are five common questions about feedback and ways to address the nuances at a distance.

How is feedback accepted?

Try as we might to give feedback in the best way, at the best time, and with the best words, how our feedback is received starts with the other person's perception. The other person decides how to take a leader's input, and its value, based on three factors:

- *Position.* If you are the boss, you have some positional power and so people will likely listen to your feedback, but not necessarily value it as highly as you might like. This is the one you have automatically, but it is the least valuable of the three. Are you relying solely on this? If so, you're likely only getting compliance.

- *Expertise.* People value feedback from people they view as knowing what they are talking about. If your team members don't recognize your experience with or knowledge of what you are giving feedback on, it will be less valued. And as a Long-Distance Leader, it may be harder for you to establish that credibility. Make it your goal for people to know your background to establish this credibility, without being arrogant or cocky. Remember that you don't have all the expertise. Maybe some feedback would be more effective coming from someone on the team who has the expertise.

- *Relationship.* We have all asked people for feedback about a situation they know little about. Why? Because we trust them and their intentions. We know that they will be honest and that their feedback is meant to help us, even if it is hard to hear. As a Long-Distance Leader, it will take more effort to build strong relationships with your team members, but it's worth the effort.

What do we give feedback on?

We must give feedback on the things that matter—on the parts of the job that are most important, make the biggest impact, and can create the most valuable results. Chances are you've been given feedback on something that seemed insignificant and petty. It's a good bet you didn't feel great about that feedback, or the person who delivered it to you—and it gets worse in a remote relationship where there is less overall interaction. Make sure you deliver feedback on what is meaningful, not just on what you can see, and if it is meaningful, make sure people see why.

What makes it helpful?

Feedback is helpful when it's clear and specific. The best ways to achieve this is to use examples, have evidence, and give the feedback based on observable behavior. If there is clear data, it reduces the length and strength of people's defensiveness. Use technology to share screens so you can both see that data. In some situations, making it observable might be harder if you haven't actually seen the behavior yourself. "Avoid telling the customer they were wrong" is more specific than "you need to be more careful about what you put in your email." Making it clear and specific, with examples, isn't just for the things that are going wrong. The same criteria apply when people do well, which leads us to the next question.

What about the balance of positive to negative feedback?

We believe, and the research backs us up, that most people don't receive enough positive feedback in the workplace—from their boss or anyone else.[1] This is even more true when people work remotely. When giving feedback over the phone, the tendency is for the feedback to become very transactional. Given that, it's likely that the "necessary" negative or corrective feedback will

> When giving feedback over the phone, the tendency is for the feedback to become very transactional.

be shared more than the positive, encouraging input. Positive feedback is just as critical, and we have to remember to include it, even if you have to write it down first to help you remember. Don't just "toss in" some fluffy positives either just to feel like you are giving balanced feedback.

People need to know (and will grow) when they know both what they are doing well and what they need to adjust. Since they are likely doing some of each, it is your job to make sure you notice and share a balanced view of what is going on.

How to deliver it?

If you are going to provide feedback, you should be prepared. Take the time to collect your thoughts, have examples ready, and be clear on what you want to share. Unfortunately, when we are well prepared, our first inclination is to start the conversation by sharing what we have prepared. Instead, open by asking them to share feedback on themselves. Questions like "How is it going from your perspective?" or "What feedback would you give yourself?" are good ways to create a conversation. If you, as the boss, go first, what is really left for them to share? If you are doing this over the phone, remember that pauses seem longer and even more uncomfortable, so you may start talking too soon. You want their input, so be patient and wait for it.

Are you looking forward?

Most all feedback is given on what has already happened—perhaps that is why it is called feed*back*. Feedback about the past is helpful and provides context and data, but for this information to be helpful, it needs to be about what comes next. Leadership coach Marshall Goldsmith calls this feed*forward*— commentary about what to be doing or changing *in the future*.[2] Again, when we are coaching and providing feedback at a distance, the risk is that we don't take ample time to make the feedback complete and connect the dots for people to see how what has passed can inform what happens next time, or confirm true understanding.

What about Performance Management?

Performance management and performance reviews matter to all your team members, regardless of where they work. As with other facets of leading at a distance, you must be more conscious, intentional, and focused on your team members to do this well.

For your remote team members, we find that the intentionality needed to think longer and think differently is difficult. Since your interactions with your remote folks are more infrequent, leaders tend to focus on the tasks—including "filling out the performance appraisal form." By now you know the problems with that approach.

We have created an online tool to assist you in doing this well. See the online resources at the end of this chapter for more information.

Getting Delegation Right

Delegation has confounded leaders for a long time. We believe the problem is less about the steps of doing the delegating, because once you have decided, for the right reasons, to delegate, it is all about teaching and coaching. If you approach delegation correctly, doing it at a distance just requires some adjustments.

What we all say about delegation

There are two phrases about delegation that nearly everyone can complete in unison in our workshops. They are:

- "If you want something done right, you should _____."
- "It would take longer to delegate [or teach someone] than it would to just _____."

In case you aren't tracking, the answers are "do it yourself."

These two statements are often used as an excuse for not delegating, and both statements are true *at this moment*. If you are thinking about delegating something you have done yourself many times, yes, you *will* do it better and faster than a first timer. But delegation isn't about the first time, it is about the long term, and it's not about you, it's about helping the individual achieve the organization's goals (notice the model—the focus on both Outcomes and Others). If you want people to succeed in doing a new task, you must think of it as an investment of time—both yours and theirs.

Delegating takes patience, time, and effort. It will likely take restraint on your part (not to step in and do it), and it will likely be even harder when doing it at a distance. Take more time up front, set a plan for check-in conversations (which will look different depending on what is being delegated, but the point of check-ins is important), and focus on the other person's success rather than getting rid of the task yourself.

There's an additional wrinkle to delegation in a remote or hybrid team environment. One of the greatest sources of tension on teams today is the perception that one person or group is getting the dirty end of the stick when it comes to tasks assigned to them. For example, it's common for the people in the office to say, "Well sure the remote workers are getting more done, because the boss comes to us for all the extra dirty work." Make sure that everyone on your team is aware of what the others are doing, and when a task is assigned and to whom. The perception of fairness is at least as important as actually being fair.

The focus

Lots of leadership books will tell you that as a leader you must delegate. Your time is precious, and if you don't delegate your plate will be overflowing and you will have no work/life balance. While we agree with the point, we believe there is an unintended consequence in that line of thinking: that delegation is something you need to do for yourself.

That is the wrong focus.

If you make delegation about something you need to do for you, you will likely do it wrong, with too little patience, and you will likely "prove" the statements we made above. In other words, as Kevin says, you won't be delegating, you will be dumping work on someone.

When you realize that delegation is about helping someone else succeed at a new task, grow in their responsibilities, and contribute to the team, and that delegation will take some time but is worth that investment, you will likely do it just fine. The person you are delegating to will likely accept the work and succeed at it, and you will have created a more flexible team too.

And when you do all that, you will lessen your load a bit too, which also is important.

Stated another way, when you keep the Three O Model in mind, by placing yourself last, delegation will work better, and you will get all the benefits you wanted.

Great (Remote) One-on-One Coaching Meetings

The heart of the coaching process is the one-on-one meeting. This is a planned time to sit down and talk about how things are going and how you can help. In the good old days you called them face-to-face meetings, but now we'll call them one-on-ones.

Many people think about the one-on-one as a status or update meeting, and we agree that is an important reason to "meet." We also believe that these planned conversations can and should include a coaching component. To make your remote one-on-ones most effective, keep the following points in mind.

Have a schedule

Talk with each team member to decide how often you will "meet." If you feel you need to meet more frequently than they want, negotiate, or start with their preferred frequency with the agreement to adjust the timing in the future as needed. Currently Kevin has eleven people reporting to him. The frequency of one-on-ones isn't the same for each person. Factors like the nature of their work, their experience and confidence with the work, the type of support he can provide, and the personal preferences of the other person all play into the frequency of these meetings.

In our experience, this frequency could be daily (though then there may be less coaching in every single meeting) up to monthly. We typically recommend scheduling them somewhere between weekly and monthly, based on the factors just described. Everything else being equal, we recommend greater frequency when people are remote. The one-on-one meeting is an important way to keep remote people connected, because in so many ways they aren't.

Use your tools

Since we are having these one-on-ones but we aren't face-to-face, we recommend making as many of them as possible as rich as possible. In other words, use webcams, screen sharing, and dashboard tools whenever possible! As we travel we have witnessed too many important calls being made in airports or hotel lobbies (or even public restrooms). These meetings are important and shouldn't be fit into a small opening on the calendar or when one of you is driving to a client meeting. They need to take place when both parties can focus on the important topic of mutual success.

Create co-ownership of the meeting

These meetings benefit both you and your team member. You want to be updated and have a chance to support, encourage, and correct people as needed, and they need direction, information, and encouragement. The meeting isn't your meeting or their meeting—it must be owned by both of you. More than a nice intellectual thing to say, this means that both parties need to take these meetings seriously, clear their calendars, come prepared, and hold the other accountable for all of this. At Intel, for example, the employees set the agenda for these meetings.[3]

Let them go first

The inherent power imbalance that exists because you are the boss means you must ensure mutual ownership of the meeting is maintained. Remember what we said earlier about letting the other person open the conversation. Kevin has messed this up many times in the past; now he has trained himself (he thinks) to stop and flip the conversation back to the other person if he starts off. Everyone wins when you have them go first. It is easier to forget this when you're more concerned about time or getting tasks done than why you are meeting in the first place.

Schedule face-to-face

When your work situation allows, make time for face-to-face conversations. You want to build the relationships then, even if it means staying an extra day or catching a later flight (or having them do the same) to build connection, and use this time to specifically have your one-on-one that would normally be at a distance. Take advantage of face time whenever you can.

Always be coaching

In the famous scene in the movie *Glengarry Glen Ross*, Alec Baldwin implores a sales team to "always be closing." We like his formula and focus on something important (but not his coaching tactics, if you have seen the movie). If you make it your mantra to "always be coaching," not just in one-on-ones but in all situations, you will be a more effective leader and reduce some of the inherent barriers that come with leading remote team members.

Informal Remote Coaching

There is more to coaching than the planned on-on-one meeting, though. While less serendipitous in a remote work environment, the best leaders/ coaches are always watchful for opportunities to engage a team member, ask a question, and provide some encouragement or correction. Kevin often uses time at the end of a team call to engage one or two team members in quick conversations, one after the other, much as you might after a real meeting in the conference room.

By recognizing that opportunity, and making it more casual in nature, he is creating these opportunities that would have otherwise been missed. Kevin does this intentionally and you can to—but you must plan and build that extra time into your calendar.

Because these informal moments are so important to performance and in creating ongoing feedback, you need to find ways to coach in informal ways and spontaneous situations better. Said in a different way, you have to find time to coach when you don't have time to coach.

The informal coaching moment

The informal coaching moment isn't scheduled, preplanned, or on anyone's calendar. It's what Thomas Peters and Robert Waterman famously called, in their bestselling book *In Search of Excellence*, "management by walking around."[4] When you are walking by, in proximity to, and popping your head into someone's office, you have the opportunity for the informal coaching moment. Specifically, the informal coaching moment includes what's going on, what's coming up, and how you can help.

For your remote team members, it's a long walk to where they are, but the point here is the same. You must create ways to engage with your folks even though you don't see them all the time. This can be done with phone call check-ins, a morning text or instant message, or any way to let them know you are around, available, and accessible. This works in both directions.

Wayne sends Kevin a quick Slack message almost every morning with a greeting and an opening for the informal conversation. Doing that is the same (regardless of who instigates it) as the hello in the break room, or the popping the head in the door on your way to your desk. Most days there's nothing to report, but occasionally it provides a moment for a quick one-on-one or a chance for either person to ask or answer a question.

Preparing for the moment

While you can (and should) be intentional about creating these moments to check in and provide encouragement and guidance, they shouldn't feel contrived or forced. If you have questions about the business, their results or project progress, or anything else, of course have a list, mental or otherwise. Be prepared, but be prepared to really engage and connect, not grill them or drill down to specific points the moment you establish contact.

Creating the moment

If you have team members on-site, you may say hello; ask them about their hobby, weekend, or family; and then use open-ended questions to shift gears from relationship building to a business check-in and coaching moment. When working remotely, use the call, text, or instant message as the way to open the door. Remember that a big part of the success of informal coaching meetings is the engagement with the other person. Start by getting them to talk about what is happening, how they are doing, and how you can help (the components of an informal coaching moment).

Here are some simple questions to start and continue the informal coaching moment:

- "What's up?"
- "How's it going?"
- "What's working?"
- "Where are you stuck?"
- "How can I help?"

These questions are short (only fifteen words in five questions!) and are open ended enough to allow the other person to point the conversation where they need it. Once the conversation is moving, you might redirect with a more specific question in context, but that will depend on how the conversation develops.

Notice one of our examples wasn't, "Do you have a minute?" There are few things more terrifying to someone working from home than an IM/text from the boss that simply asks, "Do you have a minute?" The goal isn't to catch people off guard or feel pressured or unprepared. By the time you get that person on the phone, they've already imagined every horrible scenario possible. Even if you just want to pass on good news, you may have created unintentional stress. Wayne often asks, "Do you have a moment? Nothing important, just a question." That helps set a more positive tone and reduces everyone's blood pressure.

Keep them short

For the most part, the informal coaching moment should be just that—moments, not minutes or a half hour in length. If the conversation develops and more time is needed or desired, of course you will mutually know to move the conversation forward appropriately.

Helen, in our example, has transformed her relationships and the performance and results of her team members. None of this replaces or erases the need for more formal planned performance and coaching conversations and standing one-on-ones we have discussed, but your meetings will be more productive, and likely less frequent, when you leverage informal coaching moments.

Pause and Reflect

▶ How successfully are you coaching your remote team members?

▶ Would they answer the same way?

▶ Are your remote and co-located people getting the same quality and frequency of feedback from you?

▶ How transparent are you with the full team when delegating tasks?

▶ How intentional are you in finding moments to connect with and coach your remote team members?

Online Resources

For more resources go to:

LongDistanceLeaderBook.com/Resources

For help with being successful with performance management and performance reviews request the **Remote Performance Management Tool.**

For more details on our coaching model request the **Sample Coaching Model and Description.**

Section Three Summary

So What?

- How successfully are you setting goals (at all levels) with your team?

- Would your team's answer be the same as yours? (If not, you might want to think about question 1 some more.)

- Which ideas in the areas of coaching and feedback could you implement to improve the results for you and your team?

- Are you "meeting" with your remote team members often enough and with the right preparation and intention?

Now What?

Other than spending time with the questions above, here are some actions to take, based on the ideas in this section.

- Review your goals and implementation plans, personally, with each team member and as a team.

- Have a conversation to see if people feel you are on track. If not, refocus on the goals and plans. Check your calendar. If it doesn't have any coaching on it this week, fix that right now. Find three positive, meaningful things to share with members of your team before the end of the day, then share them.

Section Four

Engaging Others

Leadership is the art of getting someone else to do something you want done because he wants to do it.

—Dwight D. Eisenhower

Section Four Introduction

As we discussed in the last section, understanding, translating, and communicating the goals of the organization is a critical part of the leadership job description. It's the outside ring of our Three O Model. Whether you want to be the best company in your niche or the most awarded Boy Scout troop in town, it all starts with understanding (and making sure everyone else understands) what needs to be done and why.

To achieve those outcomes, you must engage your team members, including their hearts and minds. Engaging others is one place where working remotely really becomes complicated and radically different than the ways we worked before.

In the "old days," people might have worked hard because the boss was watching—he or she could pop in at any moment and find them doing something they shouldn't . . . or not doing what they should. *Leading remotely requires influence more than command.* There are levels of accountability, trust, and proactive communication that, while desirable in a traditional workplace, are absolutely critical when you're not in close physical proximity.

How we engage others in a digitally connected but physically isolated world will largely determine whether you hit your goals, and how stressful it will be along the way.

Chapter 9

The "Golden Suggestion" for Working with Others

Rule 9: Communicate in the ways that work best for others rather than based on your personal preferences.

The greatest lesson you might ever
learn in this life is this: it is not about you.

—Shannon L. Alder, author

Two members of our friend Alice's project team are equally good at their jobs. They both serve the same function, and she has an equally high opinion of both. Yet when she received some feedback from her team members, one of them felt she was "micromanaging" while the other felt she could check in *more* often. How can both things be true when she maintains the same schedule with each?

Alice was confused. After all, she was following the Golden Rule. She used to do their job, and was very good at it. She was also an experienced teleworker, brilliant, and excellent at focusing and drowning out distractions until the job was done. She always wanted her manager to give her guidelines, check in infrequently, keep interactions short, and be there when she did have a question or needed help but otherwise generally stay out of her way. To Alice's mind, that's how she always wanted to be managed and therefore how she planned to work with her team.

One of the most quoted adages of all time is known as the Golden Rule: "Do unto others as you'd like them to do unto you." It's darned fine advice, and some variant of it is found in nearly every major religion and school of philosophy. It's also, when it comes to leading and communicating at a distance, slightly flawed. We're not talking about the notion that you shouldn't do or ask something of someone you wouldn't be willing to do yourself. Instead, we're challenging the notion that other people work in the same way we do and want to be managed and led the same way we like to work.

The problem is, not everyone has Alice's experience. Some people need constant short interaction to feel connected to the work and check assumptions. Others want to get their marching orders, be left alone to complete them, and would prefer to initiate the contact when they need help.

That's what was happening. One employee—newer to the team and unused to teleworking—wanted some form of contact almost daily. Sometimes there were specific questions to be addressed, sometimes that person just wanted to know they weren't alone in the universe. It took very little time, and often required only a simple instant message asking, "How's it going? How can I help?"

The other employee was tenured and a bit of an introvert. That worker preferred longer, highly structured, and less frequent discussions, usually by phone or (grudgingly) webcam. Alice often needed to initiate the conversation, which that worker took as interruptions.

One person's short, frequent check-ins can be someone else's intrusive micromanaging. Your trust in someone's ability and desire to stay out of their way may be seen as a lack of communication or even caring.

When everyone works in the same location, it's much easier to pick up the signals that tell us how to work with other people. You learn who's a morning person and who isn't. You can tell who the extroverted, chatty people are and who are the people sitting at their desk with their headphones on, just plowing through their work. When you approach their desk, you can see them welcoming the contact or the agony of yet another interruption written all over their face.

When working and leading at a distance, some of these cues are missing, so you might tend to work from your assumptions, personal preferences, and your more limited history with the other person. Similar to the Golden Rule, you lead and manage others in the way you want to be led and managed. Since humans are all different, that strategy will, by definition, limit your success.

That is why we suggest modifying the Golden Rule into the Golden Suggestion—to lead others in the way that works best for *them* makes sense. It's a suggestion because you will never be 100 percent sure what works best for them.

Putting the "Suggestion" to Work

There are a couple of ways to gather the insight you need to make that decision more confidently:

Work style analysis and profiles

You are probably pretty good at "picking up signals" from the people you work with, or you wouldn't be in a leadership role (or reading this book). Still, there are plenty of tools designed to help you identify your own preferred working and communication style and either find out (or at least get a sense of) the styles of others. Assessments like DISC, Myers-Briggs, Insights, or Strengths-Finder can help you and your team identify the areas where you mesh together, as well as where there may be sources of challenge.

Most of these tools can be administered online; others are conducted in person. No matter how and when the assessment is done, make sure there are training and resources available *after* the assessment to help apply what you (and your team) learn to real-life behaviors. Don't skip that step.

Keep in mind that these are not full psychological studies, but they can be very helpful in helping people see why one teammate needs all the details before they decide and the other will rely more on their intuition.

While we use DISC most often (and you can use our free assessment at https://discpersonalitytesting.com/ldl), we care less about which assessment you use than that you consider using one to better understand differences in communication and behavioral styles. Remember that getting a picture is far more important than which camera you use to take that picture.

Consider people's preferences

You probably have team members who prefer one communication method over another; some might prefer texting or email while others perhaps the phone. If the tool doesn't matter for the success of the message, pick the one they prefer—this in a subtle way builds trust in the relationship without negatively impacting the communication. However, if the choice of tool matters to the business outcome (e.g., you don't want someone texting a customer who is upset), as the leader you need to set an expectation, not bow to people's preference.

Ask people how they want to work with you

This sounds obvious, but were the team norms you've established built through real conversation, or did you simply tell people how—and how often—you'd communicate with them? Going back to Alice's story, frequent short check-ins may be necessary/desired for one person, while someone else doesn't want to be interrupted unnecessarily. For that second person, your "staying in touch" looks an awful lot to them like "constantly bothering."

Remember that equal does not mean the same. While you want the team to settle on norms for things like how often you'll meet in person, how often you'll hold conference calls or virtual meetings, and so on, you may need to adjust the frequency, length, and mode of communication with each person on your team.

Ask, but it might not work

Just asking doesn't always get you what you need, but it can't hurt. Remember that there's always a power imbalance between you as the leader/manager and your team members, so it's important to phrase your questions carefully. When you ask, "Is once a week often enough to check in?" the other party may read that as the boss telling them what they should say rather than as an actual request for information.

Make sure that when you're seeking this information, you phrase it as a neutral question about their preference. For example:

- "How can I help you be successful? I want to support you and help you stay on track."

- "How often would you like for us to have a one-on-one?"

You may not know what makes the other person tick, and even if you ask, the information will be filtered by your position and their level of intimidation. Again, the Golden Rule would have you do what works for you; the Golden Suggestion requires more thought and nuance, especially when leading at a distance.

Our own example

Although we are coauthors of this book, Wayne technically works for Kevin. While he'd basically be happy to never attend another team meeting, and he's fine being left alone to do his work, he does need frequent, short communication. Kevin works hard to schedule and balance team communication. The thing is, Wayne needs a *little* communication on a frequent basis to stay sane.

So, each morning there is a short instant message exchange between the two of us. Usually it consists of "good morning, anything I need to know?" Nine times out ten the answer is "no, carry on." While Kevin may not "need" that exchange, he knows that Wayne does. It makes Wayne feel connected. It doesn't take much time, and sometimes that exchange does blossom into a timely conversation or prompts meeting time to be scheduled that might otherwise have been delayed.

Does Kevin have these morning exchanges with every member of the team? Not at all. Meeting the relationship and communication needs of each team member is important, and they won't all be met in the same way.

If leading is about people choosing to follow, people must feel respected. Applying the Golden Suggestion helps you engage others in the most positive, constructive, and effective way possible. While it will help in all interactions, including with your team members down the hall, it is just harder to correctly judge the work styles, preferences, and needs of your remote team members.

Meeting the relationship and communication needs of each team member is important, and they won't all be met in the same way.

Pause and Reflect

▶ Who do you have the most communication challenges with?

▶ Based on what you just read, what is one way that person works differently than you?

▶ What behaviors or reactions confirm this for you?

▶ What is one thing you can adjust in how you work with that person to be a more effective leader?

Online Resource

For access to a free DISC assessment with an explanatory report, go to

https://discpersonalitytesting.com/ldl

Chapter 10

Understanding Politics without "Playing Politics"

Rule 10: Leading successfully requires an understanding of what people are thinking, not just what they are doing.

Politics is the art of looking for trouble, finding it everywhere, diagnosing it incorrectly, and applying the wrong remedies.

—Groucho Marx

One of the reasons Denise didn't want to become a leader was "politics." She wanted to earn her way on her merits and not have to suck up to people along the way. That had been her viewpoint her entire life—until a mentor helped her put politics in the right perspective. Now she understands there is a difference between playing political games and recognizing the relationships and interactions that can help get things done. With the help of that mentor, she changed her perspective and got promoted. Now she is trying to manage that while leading a team spread across the country.

Many of us grow pale at the word "politics"—that word is even why some people don't want to become leaders. Politics conjures up visions of Machiavellian plots, or people trying to consolidate power and advance their own agenda at the expense of the organization.

You might like to think you're above all that, that "I don't play politics," but no one can successfully function in groups without understanding the interactions, roles, and power that exists between people. The very word "politics," although usually applied to ruling a government entity, is simply the dynamics of trying to reach decisions and move an organization toward a goal.

As a leader, you have been aware of political dynamics throughout your career. You have figured out who the decision makers are, who is all talk and no action, and who to approach when you *really* need to get something done.

While we hope you aren't cynically manipulating people, you wouldn't have gotten promoted or found yourself in a leadership position without some understanding of how things do or don't work.

As we've already discussed, the job of leadership hasn't changed in the big picture, but being separated from those with whom we work or lead can present political challenges. In particular, leaders need to see and be seen. By "see," we really mean gather the information needed to understand what's going on within the organization. This means picking up conversational cues, noticing behaviors, and identifying rumors that may undermine the work.

Perhaps more importantly, you must understand at a deep level how information flows and relationships form. When we say "be seen," we refer to how others get their information about, and from, you as the leader. This may include visual cues but also your written communication, what others say about you, and how you serve as a model to the organization.

When everyone works in the same location, you get all kinds of information visually and without any additional thought or work. You immediately notice people are frowning and muttering or smiling and laughing and enjoying each other's company. Nobody needs to ask what the boss is doing—they can see when you get to work and when you leave. They can easily tell if you're easy to talk to and don't mind being questioned, and there are plenty of opportunities for people to experience that for themselves, or to at least witness those positive behaviors and create a positive impression of your leadership.

On the other hand, if you are out of sight for long periods of time, people wonder about what is happening with you. When there is a lack of information, assumptions can become gossip and rumors and take on a life of their own. Your actions, explained in a quick email, might be misinterpreted and because you don't talk to that person for days or weeks, there's no chance to recognize there's a problem with your message until Alice starts to act in ways you didn't expect.

Remember that gossip, like a mushroom, grows in the dark. It is your job to be transparent and accessible so that gossip won't fester. These challenges can be even larger if leading a project or other ad hoc team where all the remote players don't even report to you. And, of course, in the case of companies that work across borders, there are issues of local control and culture to think about. So, when you work remotely, you need to be very purposeful about how you see and are seen. How are you doing on that score?

"Seeing" More Clearly in a Virtual World

Whether in the same room or on different continents, you must consider the process of the work. Are people working well together? Does your team buy into the vision you are leading toward? Is the work moving forward at a good clip? Or are the results being delayed or held back because of communication differences or competing priorities?

These are good questions. Do you know the answers?

We're talking about gathering and interpreting information so that you have an accurate picture of how people are interacting and how that's impacting your organization's goals. In a remote world, this happens in many ways.

First, you need to be aware of how you gather information. If all your information is coming from the same three sources, or you're trying to understand how people work together strictly from email threads, you are giving yourself limited data on which to base decisions. Consider gathering information more widely and in a variety of ways, then process that data into a clear, accurate picture of what's going on around you. Ask more people, scan more sources, and be more alert on conference calls and virtual meetings to get a clearer picture of reality.

When working remotely, the written word takes on far greater importance. Texts, reports, emails, and IMs are how you'll get information from people who may be asleep when you're working. Read more than what the documents say, but note the tone, tenor, and the frequency too. Ask yourself, does the information come proactively or do I have to constantly track that information down?

We'll get specific about tools and techniques to accomplish this, but for now let's agree that you need a good sense of what's going on around you.

Being Seen

You gather information and develop your worldview from what you see around you, but so do the people you work with. How people see you is important. And whether you realize it or not, as the boss, they are paying close attention. They are looking for clues to answer questions like:

- Do you care about them?

- Do you care about the work?

- What work is most important?

- Can you be trusted?

- Who are your favorites?

- Do you give preferential treatment to one group (or to the people in the office)?

- Do you do the things you ask them to do?

Everyone you interact with is searching through their own experiences and results to decide how they should interact with you. As a leader, be more aware of the impressions you make. If people know you mostly as a signature on an email and not a real person, you are constraining their ability to get a positive, accurate impression of you and what you're trying to accomplish—and why. In the absence of hard evidence, people tend to fill in the blanks—and often not in positive ways. If the leader isn't visible to people, it leaves plenty of room for rumor, gossip, and misinterpretation of messages.

As a leader, are you being seen often enough? How are you visible to your team? And what are they seeing (and how do you know)?

Understanding Politics in Your Organization

You can't be everywhere at once, and with a bigger span of control the sheer amount of communication needed can be overwhelming—and that is before your folks are spread from here to who-knows-where. Still, you must be aware of how your organization works and where your information comes from.

Whether it's a multinational corporation or the PTA committee you chair, a leader must understand the roles involved in making everything come together and identify the people critical to success.

Whether it's a multinational corporation or the PTA committee you chair, a leader must understand the roles involved in making everything come together and identify the people critical to success.

As a leader, you're not expected to obsess about every disagreement or become paranoid about whether someone is after your job. You are expected, though, to be aware of relationships and dynamics that can support or hinder your efforts and support or undermine the group's success. Be aware that these factors are constantly changing, and you need to mindfully assess how things stand with your team from time to time.

Here is an exercise to help you assess the relationships and communication in your organization and help identify potential blind spots. They might also be worth discussing with your team.

- *Draw an organization chart by memory, then compare it to the "official" version.* Did you remember all the groups? Did some slip your mind? Are there places where you know there are roles but don't know the names of the people involved?

- *Compare the official version to what's really going on.* Can you identify the decision makers and influencers in that group? You know from experience that job titles don't confer expertise or trust among peers. Do you know who has the ear of their peers and how well they're working together?

Pause and Reflect

▶ Where are your relationships strong and positive?

▶ Where do you need to improve relationships?

▶ Are those gaps with individuals or with entire groups and teams of people?

▶ How much do you trust the information you are currently getting?

▶ What is the cause of those gaps?

▶ How does being remote impact these challenges, and what can you do about it?

Chapter 11

Understanding and Building Trust at a Distance

Rule 11: Building trust at a distance doesn't happen by accident.

Few things can help an individual more than to place responsibility on him, and to let him know that you trust him.

—Booker T. Washington

Liz has always prided herself in being a leader who could build trust—it was part of what made her a successful leader. But once she began leading a remote team, she felt at a loss. She wanted to build the sort of positive relationships she always had, but now she had these new team members she didn't know and seldom saw. She struggled until she began to understand the dynamics of trust differently. Once she had a bigger picture, she proceeded to be more successful with her new remote team.

Trust is invaluable to leaders. We need to be able to trust the people we lead, and they certainly need to trust us. Jim Kouzes and Barry Posner have written widely on the importance of trust, as have countless others.[1] At least as importantly, your experience tells you that when people trust you, and you trust them, things work better, more work gets done, and it gets done faster.

When working remotely, it's foolish to say that trust is *more* important than when you are all working in the same location. What's different when working remotely is that trust is harder to build and more easily broken. Even worse, the results of that lack of trust may not be immediately visible, and the damage may be irreparable. Your project may have fallen way behind schedule, your team may have become dysfunctional, or key employees may leave the organization and you didn't see any of it coming.

The Trust Triangle

Whether we're talking about a romantic couple, your circle of friends, or that project team you inherited, trust is built—and destroyed—in the same ways. There have been many studies of the subject, and plenty of models created. At the Remote Leadership Institute, we have read literally hundreds of books and research articles on trust and have identified three components necessary for high levels of trust to exist: common purpose, competence, and motives (figure 10). The more alignment of these three components, the more trust will exist.

Figure 10   The Trust Triangle

The Trust Components in Action

Say you have a friend you play cards with regularly. If you are connected by that *common purpose*, you have trust in that area (you both love playing the game and enjoy each other's company). If you both have *competence* at the game (you both know the rules, have a similar level of skill and strategy, and can play the game fairly) and see that in each other, trust will further build. And as long as you both feel your *motives* are congruent (you want to play the game and see who wins), trust will be high in this area too. But if you find out that your friend is cheating—that his motives for playing the game aren't the same as yours—trust will be reduced. At best, you won't want to play cards with that person anymore, and at worst you may never speak to them again. And the components of the Trust Triangle explain it all.

Here are some leadership examples, in the form of questions.

- *Common purpose.* Do you and the people you lead have the same purpose? Are you "pulling on the same end of the rope"? If people get the sense that you are not sincere in your beliefs, or they begin to question the organization's goals and behaviors, this may suffer.

- *Competence.* Do you believe that the people you lead are competent? Are they capable of doing what you ask of them? Do your employees believe that you can deliver on your promises? If sales targets are ridiculously high and people come to believe that you don't know what you're talking about, there will be a lack of trust. Does your project team understand all you are doing to coordinate and create results even when the project frustration level is high?

- *Motives.* Finally, you might all have the same goals, and everyone is technically capable of acting appropriately, but are they willing to go the extra mile? Do you have your employees' backs, or will you always side with the company? Do you do what you say you'll do, or do people suspect you're just telling them what they want to hear?

All these questions and situations apply regardless of where everyone works. Like most everything else, the factors for building trust are the same as when you're together, but people think about it differently and it becomes harder when you aren't near each other.

How Working Remotely Impacts Trust

In a perfect world, there should be no difference between whether you work with someone down the hall or far from them. You both have jobs to do. You do yours, they do theirs, and neither party loses any sleep about what's happening. Yet in our work with clients, we hear all kinds of concerns from team members rooted in a lack of trust:

- "How will I know they're working if I can't see them?"

- "The people in the home office get all the attention and promotions."

- "The people working from home have it great. They don't have to do all the dirty little jobs and the manager leaves them alone to get their work done. We are in eyesight, so she comes to us first and leaves the teleworkers alone."

One of the most dramatic stories we've encountered took place when Wayne was discussing the use of webcams as a means of building trust. One of the participants in a session informed him that they didn't use webcams, and in fact it was common practice to put tape or sticky notes over the cameras, even when they weren't in use. When asked why, the answer was "because they only want us to use webcams to make sure we're working, and we don't want them [management] spying on us."

How bad is the level of trust in an organization if people are refusing to use communication tools because they believe the organization is watching them at all times? On the other hand, if your organization is doing that, well let's just say trust is a legitimate issue, and we'd encourage you to work on that as soon as possible.

An example

Helen has two coworkers. She's worked with Gretchen in the past and knows that even though Gretchen doesn't say much in meetings, she's diligent, and when she does speak, it's always useful. Also, in all the time Helen has known her, she's never seriously missed a deadline or failed to honor a commitment. Helen trusts Gretchen implicitly.

Meanwhile, Rajesh is new to the team and he and Helen have never met in person. She knows nothing about him except that he's occasionally spoken on conference calls and seems smart enough, but she notices he missed his last deadline.

Who does Helen trust less? The problem (probably) doesn't lie solely with Rajesh. Anyone could miss a deadline, but Helen is making her judgment about his competence, alignment to the group, and motivation based on a very small amount of data. If she's a naturally trusting person, she might cut him some slack, but if she's paranoid, or in a hurry, or just in a bad mood, she's going to go with the person she *knows* she can trust. She might even decide she's never going to Rajesh for help for anything.

In real life

This happens in remote teams all the time. When you send out an instant message cry for help, Joanne always answers in a hurry, so you note that she's obviously motivated to help. When you send a similar IM to Bob, he takes all day to respond, so you assume he doesn't care if you live or die. That's likely unfair. Maybe Bob has been in a meeting all day or wanted to make sure he got the absolute best answer before responding, but all you know is that with the data available, you've decided to trust Joanne more than Bob, and over time she becomes your go-to for answers.

Trust is evidence-based. Without evidence, we must guess at whether we can trust people. If you like to assume positive intent, that works for a while, but what do you do when something happens to shake your trust? For most people it's easier to damage trust than rebuild it.

For most people it's easier to damage trust than rebuild it.

When working remotely, you have fewer opportunities to assess whether someone's really aligned with your purpose, is competent at their job, and is as motivated as you are. When you work in the same location, you see them come in early and leave late, you see them taking notes in meetings. You know that if you have a question about X, Inez is the person to talk to. But when you don't really know the people you work with and have few opportunities to interact with them, it's difficult to build a strong, lasting, trusting work relationship.

Intentionally Building Trust at a Distance

Trust can be built at a distance, but it doesn't happen by accident. Give people opportunities to see that everyone is aligned on the three corners of the Trust Triangle: purpose, competence, and motives. Creating and helping build this alignment with the three corners of the Trust Triangle is an important part of your job. Once people know who they're working with and how smart their fellow team members are, and that they are all headed to the same destination, they will help others out when needed or asked, which builds trust.

When working remotely, the team doesn't often interact as much as they would in person. Frequently, communication goes through you as the leader, and the team doesn't have nearly as many chances to see each other in action. That's why a Long-Distance Leader does some very practical things to help build trust as a team and between team members. Consider this list:

- *Use meetings strategically.* One of the unfortunate side effects of our 24/7 world is that time has become too precious to waste. Unfortunately, many leaders treat meetings as something to be done as quickly as possible, with no wasted time. Too often that means making meetings transactional and short. The nature and flow of a conference call or a webmeeting makes this even more true. Yet those meetings may be the only time the team speaks to each other as a group. Build in time for people to really see how smart the team is. You could try showcasing one person per meeting, letting them talk about their work, or highlighting their strengths for them ("If you guys have a question about Excel, Inez can help"). Or do quick introductions each week, allowing people to get answers to questions or challenges they face. Nothing shows motivation like someone helping solve a problem. Use all the keys to great meetings, including agendas, but remember that with a remote team these meetings do more than communicate and get the work done—they are a time when trust can be built.

- *Share praise in public.* As a leader, you know that positive feedback is important (and we talked much more about this and feedback in general in chapter 8). Unfortunately, in a virtual world that might happen one-on-one. That makes the person feel good, but the rest of the team doesn't hear what a fine job they did on the Jackson account or how hard they worked to help everyone meet that deadline. We need to help the team learn each other's strengths, talents, and efforts.

- *Delegate in public.* When assigning tasks, the perception of fairness is as important as equality itself. Often remote teams don't know what others are working on. This can lead to a sense that "those folks" are being spared the dirty jobs you're making others do. When you delegate or assign projects, let the whole team know who's doing what. Though you likely won't do the delegation on your call/meeting ("Adrienne, I want you to . . ."), you might help more than you know by letting the team know that you have handed that off to Adrienne.

- *Intentionally create opportunities to get to know and build trust with each other.* Leaders can help their people get to know each other by intentionally mixing up teams, assigning mentors, and delegating some of the training between team members so that people get the chance to interact with teammates they might not otherwise work closely with. Don't sacrifice opportunities to build team trust in the interest of "getting back to work."

- *Use technology to build relationships.* We all work best with people we know, like, and trust. But how do we get to know each other? Synchronous tools like webcams allow people to put faces to names. Research at DePaul University shows that when we know the other person's face, there's a decrease in negative behaviors like lying, exclusion, and being overly aggressive.[2] Help your team put faces to names. We will say it again: encourage the use of webcams, especially one-on-one. You can also use asynchronous tools like SharePoint to showcase task status and expertise. If your team is large or spread across many time zones, consider Q & A forums, where people who don't speak to each other can still offer help and insight to their teammates.

- *If you see something, say something.* There are plenty of signs that trust may be an issue on the team. If you're suddenly being deluged with email (e.g., being copied on every communication), that could be a sign of trouble. It might be their way of letting you know what they are working on, or perhaps they don't trust the other person and think including you into the email thread will ensure a response. When you see behavior that might indicate a problem, be proactive to identify what's really happening, help people clarify the situation, help build connection, reduce conflict, and if necessary reset expectations.

Remember that trust is easily broken and hard to mend. It also can't be done unilaterally. Frequent, candid conversation with both your team and the individual members can help avoid problems. As Napoleon once said, "If you want to avoid war, avoid the thousand little pinpricks that lead to war."

Pause and Reflect

▶ Do you see signs of eroded trust on your team? What are they?

▶ Look at the Trust Triangle. Which factor(s) seem to be out of whack?

▶ What can you do as a leader to address this issue?

Online Resource

For more resources go to:

LongDistanceLeaderBook.com/Resources

and request the **Trust Thermostat Tool.**

Chapter 12

Choosing the Right Communication Tools

Rule 12: Identify the leadership results you need, then select the communication tool to achieve them.

The medium is the message because it is the medium that shapes and controls the search and form of human associations and actions.

—Marshall McLuhan, professor and media critic

Theresa laments that it used to be easy when everyone worked in the office. You had face-to-face communication, meetings, and some email. Now, with people working everywhere, the tools she needs to master require two hands to count. The problem is, some of the tools she isn't sure how to use, some she has never seen used well, and some, well, she just doesn't like. Since the face-to-face is out, she leans on email far too often, even though she knows it sometimes gets her into problems.

We've been saying throughout the book that long-distance leadership is *mostly* the same as traditional leadership except for the pesky technology. That's an awfully small hinge swinging a terribly big door.

Most of you have a complicated relationship with technology. If you've been around long enough, you may have gone through two or three generations of tools already. You realize that while new technology may solve one problem, nothing fixes every issue (and sometimes creates a whole new set of unexpected headaches). And even if you are competent with the current tools, you know they continue changing.

Three things are most assuredly true:

- Things change quickly when it comes to communication technology.

- Unless you own the company, the decision over what's available to you is probably not yours alone.

- No one has explicitly set expectations on the best ways to communicate with your team (and if you don't know, your team members don't either).

- Further, picking the right tools impacts more than just simply delivering information. Choosing the right tool involves considering how you want to get your message across and how can you can receive feedback on that message effectively. From a "see and be seen" perspective, choosing the right tool for the job is critical.

The available tools, and the way they're used, also impact how we create and nurture trust. If your team is scattered across time zones but the only way they really must talk to each other is synchronous, how are the people in India expected to demonstrate their competence and motivation to the people in Los Angeles, who are asleep when they're doing their best work?

In that case, using SharePoint to ask important questions, and allowing people to answer them online when convenient, might get them comfortable with the tool. It might even be better than having another meeting. We want to help you improve your judgment and make better tool selection decisions. It starts with a simple tool that we use in many of our programs to help people focus their thinking about which tool to use when (and how).

In 2001, the Swiss/German researcher Bettina Büchel created a simple matrix that we think explains this concept as well as anything we've seen (figure 11).[1] In order for communication to be effective and appropriate, you want to strike the right balance between richness and scope.

Let's look at what this model means in your daily work as a Long-Distance Leader.

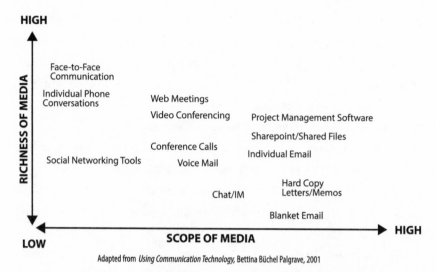

Adapted from *Using Communication Technology,* Bettina Büchel Palgrave, 2001

Figure 11   Richness and Scope in Communication

Richness

True communication is more than simply understanding the content of a message, regardless of how it's transmitted. We all know humans communicate in multiple ways. Our tone of voice, the expression on our faces, our body language, and the word choice we use all help us interpret a seemingly simple message.

When someone says "I'm fine," are they really? Maybe they can't look you in the eye as they say it, or the way they say it is a clue that they don't really believe everything is good. If you're next to them, and you can gather all those clues, you can assess if they really are fine or if you need to probe further to make sure there isn't something more you need to know.

With Büchel's model, the best example of rich communication is a one-on-one meeting over coffee. You and the other person are in physical proximity, you can see and hear each other, and you're getting all the nonverbal, visual, and social cues you need to interpret the other person's message. And you can ensure that yours is understood and accepted as well.

The problem is that these perfect circumstances rarely happen as a Long-Distance Leader. Beyond the obvious distance challenges, both time and the sheer number of people involved impact this too. If the group is large, for example, even if you're face-to-face, people may not speak up or ask questions. As the group size grows, it is very common for the communication to become a broadcast, with people holding questions until the end rather than those questions emerging organically—if they ask them at all. If you've ever been on a teleconference or webmeeting and asked, "Any questions?" only to be met with the sound of crickets, you've experienced this phenomenon.

Richness suffers over time and space. Twenty-four hours after a meeting, if you ask two people who've been part of the same conversation what they took away, you're likely to get very different interpretations. It's impractical to get face-to-face every time we need to communicate with somebody. In fact, with people scattered all over the place, it defies the laws of physics, not to mention economics! So every time we pick up the phone or fire off an email rather than get in the car, or hold a videoconference instead of hopping on a plane, we're sacrificing richness in favor of scope.

Scope

That need to account for time and distance is where scope comes in. Email is the perfect example of a tool with great scope. Thousands of people receive the same message at the same time (theoretically, at least). You can't see the reactions of your reader, hear their wails of anguish or shouts of joy, or answer their questions in real time. You don't know if you've been understood correctly or if people have bought in. And let's be honest, you don't even know if they've read the darned thing.

That's not to say that richness is superior to scope. The ability to reference past communication and make information consistent across readers and locations is important. We also know that if you've spent three days apologizing for a message it took thirty seconds to write, you understand that scope carries its own set of limitations and constraints.

Finding the Right Mix

If you look at the matrix in figure 11, you'll see that nearly every method of communication strikes some balance of richness versus scope. To have rich one-on-one conversations, you may need to sacrifice time and efficiency. You can save time by dashing off an email, but you do so at the risk of being misinterpreted, or people having questions they need answers to before they can implement your suggestion.

Too often Long-Distance Leaders are so busy doing the job, they aren't as mindful as they need to be about which tools they use and how effective they are. Remember the Remote Leadership Model in chapter 4? As a leader, be mindful of your messages and communication goals, then choose the right tool for the task.

Webmeetings are a good example. Let's say you have Skype for Business as your daily collaboration tool. In figure 11, webmeetings are in the middle ground—fairly rich, with good scope. In fact, depending on how they are used, they can be quite high in richness (e.g., one-on-one video calls, coaching and training) or have terrific scope (the dreaded but often useful "all hands meeting"). But generally you are sacrificing one factor for the other based on how you use the tool.

If you need to brainstorm effectively, you might want to have small groups using webcams and full participation with the online whiteboard. You even want to record the meeting for later use or to include those who couldn't attend. That leads to surprisingly rich communication.

On the other hand, if you're not using webcams and have a hundred people online, you might get your message out (high scope!) but will have little real chance to engage people, get input, answer questions in real time, or gauge your participants' reactions.

This doesn't make that application wrong; it might be the best way to communicate the message at hand. The point is to be mindful of what you're trying to get across, to whom, and how "richly" it needs to be done.

Often leaders choose one tool over the other for both good and bad reasons. Situationally relying on email and text messages may make sense when you are traveling and crossing time zones, but if the message is sensitive, complex, or easily misinterpreted, are you sacrificing effectiveness for convenience? Similarly, if you're coaching an employee on the phone, is it because that's the only way to have that conversation, or because one or both of you are uncomfortable with webcams and would rather not use them? (Even though it would be incredibly helpful for you to see each other's facial expressions and body language.)

Long-Distance Leaders can't avoid this important new part of the job. You must be aware of the tools at your disposal, understand their advantages and disadvantages, and then use them to their maximum potential.

Pause and Reflect

Look at figure 11. Ask yourself:

▶ Which tools are you and your team using well?

▶ Which tools do you default to?

▶ Which tools are you and your team not using well?

▶ Are there tools you don't have that would be helpful?

▶ Are there tools you have that you're not utilizing due to a lack of training or knowledge?

▶ If you used those tools, how might the way you communicate and build trust be impacted (positively and negatively)?

▶ What are you going to do about it?

Chapter 13

Technology Tips for the Long-Distance Leader

Rule 13: Maximize a tool's capabilities or you'll minimize your effectiveness.

A sufficiently advanced technology should be indistinguishable from magic.

—Arthur C. Clarke,
futurist and science fiction writer

James is surprised when he realizes how many communication tools he has at his disposal, and how few of them he uses or is comfortable with. He remembers the days when the big decision was choosing between voice mail and email. Considering the challenges he and his team face, he is sure some of these new tools hold answers but doesn't know where to start, which ones to use, or where to focus his limited time to learn more. Until he moves beyond this confusion, his frustration will grow, and his team's results will suffer.

Many leaders have a difficult relationship with electronic communication tools. As we've pointed out already, this is a challenge for the Long-Distance Leader, because so much is mediated by digital communication. As we've also pointed out, your focus should be on the *what* instead of the *how*—you need to accomplish what needs to be done, and technology is something you can't ignore.

Give yourself permission to acknowledge that some of this may be new and uncomfortable. Leaders, particularly senior leaders, struggle to use technology successfully for three reasons:

- *There's no pain.* They have been very successful without using these tools in the past, so they either discount their importance or resist learning to use them.

- *It doesn't seem "natural."* Most of them are not "digital natives." They are often older and less technically savvy than others on their teams.[1] This can often make them feel incompetent, or at least less confident than they'd like to be, and thus avoid using many of the available tools.

- *It keeps changing.* It is true that technology changes so fast many are too busy trying to get the job done to be aware of all the latest gadgets and innovations. This can create a vicious cycle of getting further and further behind in utilizing the available tools to maximize communication and organizational results.

Remember this: *not* using these tools isn't a viable option. When you realize you must build trust, communicate clearly, and have productive meetings, you need to use the technology at your disposal. That requires choosing the right tool for the right job (by balancing richness and scope) and then using the chosen tool as effectively as possible. If not, you are trying to do hard work with one hand tied behind your back.

Be honest with yourself—you may not be an expert in the use of one or more of the technology tools available to you. In fact, research shows you're probably not. Two MIT/Sloane Cap Gemini Studies show an important paradox.[2] Leaders who use and are comfortable with technology are rated consistently higher in other leadership areas than those who don't. Yet a huge number—a big majority—don't feel comfortable or confident using the tools themselves. If you need technology to do the job, but don't use it well, if at all, you're working under assumptions that are no longer true, but literally missed the memo.

The good news is you don't have to be the biggest power-user on the team. You *do* need to leverage what's at your disposal well enough to accomplish your goals and maintain your credibility. Think about it this way: you know what you need to communicate, so you must choose the best tools and use them effectively to make the communication happen.

In this chapter, we're going to look at types of tools and general categories without getting too specific. Partly, this is because we are platform-neutral—we work with most all the tools to help our clients succeed. Practically, though, we won't get specific because the cycle time in communication technologies is less than six months.

By the time you read this, a specific feature or brand name may be completely different, so we'll talk generically. What you need to know is that 90 percent of collaboration platforms have the same features; they are just called different things and labeled differently. As an important example, whatever platform you are using, you likely have a whiteboard feature. You need to know that is true, that you can use it, and that you can learn how to use it appropriately no matter what the platform.

Before we get to the tools, let's make a clear distinction between two types of communication so that you can use each to your best advantage.

- *Asynchronous communication* allows you to get the information when you need it. In a distributed workplace, a central repository of on-demand information is needed. A virtual "file room," with information stored in a variety of ways, is critical. People who miss a meeting or are sleeping while work goes on in another part of the world can receive the same information the same way when they need it.

- *Synchronous communication* happens live—at the same time for everyone involved. It's the style you're most familiar—and most comfortable with—since you've been doing it since you drew your first breath. However, in today's dispersed workplace it is nearly impossible to all be together at the same time (virtually or in the same room).

Here's why this distinction is important. Think about when leaders call a virtual meeting—everything tends to stop. Work that maybe deserves a higher priority gets put on hold. Now this meeting is an impediment to that work and becomes an interruption rather than an asset.

When it comes to getting work done, technology can be both an enabler and a barrier. When the right tool is used in the right way, there is transparency, accountability, and the ability to cross time and space.

The list that follows is by no means exhaustive because again, new products emerge every day. Stop worrying/complaining about the specific tools your IT department has given you. Chances are, what you have will *get the job done*. And if you use what you have well, you'll be fine. If you are really missing something on this list, share this chapter with (or buy a copy of the book for) your IT department manager.

Asynchronous Tools

When we think about workplace communication, it's natural to think of two or more people literally "speaking" to each other at the same time. In our 24/7, dispersed workplace, where distance and time zones often dictate that we're on different schedules, we have come to rely more and more on tools that don't require all parties to be present at the same time. For example:

Video and recorded messages

Leaders need to see and be seen. Often, we think of asynchronous tools as mostly text-based (message boards, emails), but you can add richness to even casual announcements. Video allows you to add a visual component to your communication. Rather than a broadcast voice mail, it is almost as easy to push "record" and use video. It's nice to have high-resolution, well-produced video for big, important announcements, but with the ability of smartphones and the widespread use of Facebook, Snapchat, and other programs, there's no excuse for you not to show your face on occasion. In fact, casual interaction is as important to building trust as a big production.

You might store the recordings on your network (more on this in a minute), but there are also plenty of video services where you can have a secure place to store video, or your IT group can set up a place where only your people can access them.

If you don't like seeing yourself on video or are self-conscious about using webcams, get over yourself. The number one factor in whether a team uses a tool is if their boss uses it. If you're not using your webcam regularly, don't expect your team will either, even if you have told them how important it can be.

Common file locations

Imagine a file room where every document your team creates is stored, only you don't have to go searching through dusty boxes to find them, and identifying the latest version is as simple as clicking a link. Tools like SharePoint, Google Docs, Basecamp, and other products allow a permanent, easily accessible and searchable central warehouse for information.

For the leader, it's easy to achieve transparency when people can access all your communication—newsletters, email blasts, and other written and recorded material—on demand. Even if most people won't take advantage of these tools, and it may take some work to get them to use them at all, the fact that you've made the information available is a big step in building trust and holding yourself accountable for your commitments.

Email

Yes, email is an asynchronous tool (although too often it isn't used that way). If you send an email, then sit drumming your fingers waiting for a response, *you're using it wrong*. In fact, you're putting people in an uncomfortable position and perhaps killing productivity. Imagine what your team may be thinking when you send that email. Do you want them to drop what they're doing and respond immediately? Is replying to you more important than meeting a deadline or commitment to another team member? If you need an instant response, consider a more synchronous tool like the phone, instant messaging, or a text message.

Email is best used when:

- *You need greater scope.* You have many people who need the same message at the same time (delivered in the same way).

- *You need a permanent record.* Email is great for creating a permanent record of what has been communicated. Just ask any lawyer. If you don't want a permanent record, don't use email. Remember, it is the law—email can be subpoenaed.

- *The message is complete.* Try using the "head, heart, hands" method. Give them the information you want to share (appeals to their logic), what it means to them (showing empathy and understanding), and then be clear about what you want them to *actually do* as a result of the new information (action steps and time frame). This way, the reader will understand the facts, you'll connect with them better on an empathic and emotional level (which will increase buy-in or encourage questions and feedback), and answer the important question, "So what do I do now?"

Synchronous Tools

Of course, even when people can communicate live and in the moment, they are often not in the same physical location. That's where synchronous tools come in to play.

Webcam and video chat

We're not talking about recorded messages here (although certainly, most video conversations can be easily recorded and stored). Webcam and video are really underrated for everyday communication. It is the ultimate remote one-on-one, see-and-be-seen tool. Using webcam on a regular basis serves many uses for both the leader and the members of the team.

Many people think that webcam is used best to "broadcast" messages, and it's certainly useful for that, but it is probably more useful in one-on-one situations. It's more comfortable for people to use their webcam one-on-one rather than the whole team, regardless of the tool you use. And really, if you think about the value of "rich" communication, isn't it those personal conversations where body language, tone of voice, and eye contact are most critical?

For your team member, this is a chance to communicate effectively with you. Remember, they want to see and hear you as richly as possible, and they need to communicate their ideas, concerns, and information to you in an effective manner too. Hearing someone agree to take action on the phone isn't the same as seeing the look of excitement—or abject horror—on their face when they do it. This also allows them to see you as a real person, not some disembodied name on an email or an unapproachable character from a recorded video. And if they see you in your AC/DC T-shirt from home or watch you try to work from an airport . . . that's not such a bad thing. You're human, after all.

For you as the leader, seeing the people you are speaking with is valuable on three levels:

- *Improving communication.* You are communicating to gain and share information and/or clarify next steps. It's important that you know you've made your point and the outcome will be what you want and expect. Without the visual cues, you may make a suggestion that sounds like a command and then don't get the feedback needed to question, adjust, or even decide it wasn't such a hot idea to start with.

- *Reducing isolation.* Not only do you *feel* isolated as a leader, in a virtual world you really *are* isolated. The more richly we can connect with other people, the stronger the bonds and the less alone we feel. The loneliness you feel may well be felt by the members of your team too.

- *Building trust.* The richer the communication you have, the easier it is to build trust with others. Conversely, in the absence of the visual clues, the development of trust can be slowed or more easily broken.

Using a webcam doesn't need to be a big deal. It's often the push of a button on whatever device you happen to be using. It can be as simple as Face-Time or Facebook Live, or part of your work tools like Skype. Use the tools you have, but use them.

One good way to overcome resistance to using webcams is to form a new habit. Whenever possible, schedule meetings with this question: "Do you want to talk by phone or webcam?" Just leave it open ended. Many people will jump at the chance to connect with you. It will also give you the appearance of comfort with the technology (which may or may not be true, but who's to know?), which adds to your credibility and transparency.

Since we're being transparent, here's a story that took place at the Kevin Eikenberry Group a few years ago. Kevin was convinced that using webcams would add value to our conversations, so he insisted everyone have webcams. Not surprisingly, there was some resistance, so rather than insist every conversation be visual, he allowed people to decide if and when they used their cameras. Some did, some didn't. But there were times when he felt video would aid the discussion, so when the conversation was critical or the subject complex or important, he'd ask people to be on camera. So far, so good, right?

The unintended consequence of this, though, was people began to wonder that if Kevin wanted to talk to them on webcam, they might be in trouble or the news was bad. After all, if they usually could decide, but if Kevin overrode the choice, then a request to be on webcam couldn't be good news. After some trial and error, our policy now is to use webcams often for both casual and important communication. Some people use it frequently, some use it as little as they can, but it's now no longer a big deal (at least Kevin hopes not).

Text messaging (SMS)

Text messaging and instant messaging (IM) are both synchronous, text-based tools and often get grouped together—but they are separate tools that can and should be used in different ways.

Texting is useful because it utilizes the device your people are most likely to have on them at any time day or night: their mobile phones. Therefore, when a message must have great scope (either a large audience or speed is of the essence), it works well.

Of course, texting generally works only on mobile phones, not on other devices. This means people must have their phones handy to get (and respond to) the message.

Since text messages are often read in a hurry, they are frequently misinterpreted. According to Verizon, 85 percent of people admit to answering texts in the bathroom[3]—our studies suggest the other 15 percent aren't entirely truthful. This makes sending a text a good method for quick attention-getting messages but not particularly useful (and perhaps a problem) when the message requires details or nuance.

Remember these things about texting:

- *Texting can work for business.* It's how a good portion of your team functions in everyday life.

- *You have positional power.* This makes every texted request or demand on their time feel like a command, whether you mean it that way or not. Proper tone and etiquette here are essential.

- *Texting is best used when the message is time sensitive.* Most people are now trained like Pavlov's dogs to respond immediately to a text. If you respect people's personal time and expect them to check messages only at certain hours, don't send a text. They'll stop what they're doing and check. It had better be worth it to them. If they don't see it as such, beware—you might be seen as a micromanager or a command-and-control leader.

If someone is working at home and you send this text—"Do you have a minute?"—most people will respond "yes," whether it's true or not, because you're the boss. What might be a legitimate request for information (you really want to know if they have time for this conversation and don't want to interfere with higher priorities) doesn't feel like there is an option to them. If what you're asking is "do you have time to talk?" always let people know that it's an actual request. Instead of "do you have a minute?" say something more like, "I have a meeting coming up and need some information. Do you have time to talk, or when is a good time for you?" Yes, it takes a little longer, but it provides much clearer communication as an actual question of curiosity rather than an unspoken demand.

Instant messaging

Instant messaging tends to be part of a larger communication package and is designed to cross platforms. For example, we can only text from our mobile phones, but we can use Slack (our IM tool) from all our devices.

While it's easy to get attention with a text, and possibly a simple answer to a simple question, instant messaging has several advantages:

- *There's a real keyboard.* Your kids may have double-jointed thumbs, but most of us will type more clearly and with greater detail on a real keyboard.

- *You are less likely multitasking.* Whereas texting can be done on the run, prolonged IM conversations require concentration.

- *People turn it off.* When the message isn't time sensitive, IM is better than a text because people can turn it off. Generally, they look at IM as work related and have an easier time closing the application and getting the messages when they log on.

- *It's more integrated with work.* Instant messaging platforms allow you easier access to files, email, and other ways to pass information. Although you *can* link documents in text, it's certainly easier to send an attachment by IM or flip to a document on your computer screen and copy and paste.

Generally speaking, IM is great for synchronous, detailed conversations that require reference to other information.

Telephone and conference calls

Although the phone is the tool you "grew up with" in the business world, it isn't always the most effective way to communicate. Phones are portable, talking on them is quick, and you can get very rich verbal and vocal cues. Plus, now everyone has their phone tethered to themselves 24/7.

There are also disadvantages to using the phone. Sometimes people can't hear you well, are taking the call where they can't speak openly, or are multitasking. Concentration during the blaring of airline announcements, while merging on the freeway, or while waiting for the barista to announce that their double-caramel soy latte with no foam is ready can be sorely lacking.

Teleconferences are notoriously bad for getting equal input from people—or any input at all. It seems someone's always over-contributing, and it's not always the people you want to hear from. Conversely, it's easy for people to hide and not participate at all. This challenge can be overcome, but only if you actively seek their engagement.

While we don't want to throw the phone or conference calls off our list of options, especially for speed and getting to the right people, there may be richer, better ways to conduct that piece of business, such as the next tool on our list.

Webmeetings

These tools have become very good alternatives to conference calls and one-on-one telephone chats, with one major caveat: they need to be utilized effectively, and to date that isn't always true. If we accept the common wisdom that people use only 20 percent of the available features, we can assume that these tools are woefully underutilized.

As of this writing, there are over one hundred webmeeting-style tools in the marketplace. We aren't expert on all of them, and you don't have to be either. You just need to know that most of them have the same critical features in common, that these features exist, and how they add value to your meetings. These features are:

- Webcams
- Whiteboards to capture vital information and enhance brainstorming and collaboration
- Chat to generate input and ensure people get heard
- Polling or surveying
- File transfer and saving for sharing information in real time

If you don't know about these features, talk to someone in your organization or on your team who uses them well. If you're going to use them in your everyday work, it will be worth getting that person to serve as a mentor.

Though it is important to know these functions exist so you can use them to make your meeting as rich and collaborative as it can be, there's no law that says you have to actually *run* every meeting yourself. In fact, minding the minutiae of a webmeeting can be a distraction that results in dead air, poor time management, and less-than-satisfactory outcomes.

Here's how those distractions impact us during a meeting. Imagine you're driving in an unfamiliar neighborhood, looking for an address. It's pouring down rain. What do you do? You turn down the radio so you can *see* better. It's natural—our brains can only handle so much stimulation, and we tend to shut off the functions that don't really matter. With webmeetings, we often default to using as few features as possible because we feel overwhelmed. That keeps the entire tool from being as useful as it could be.

Even if you know what your meeting should look like and how to use the various functions to accomplish those goals, it can seem overwhelming to do all that clicking. Instead, have someone else "drive"—i.e., be responsible for making sure whatever's on the whiteboard is spelled correctly and that everyone can see the slides. That way you're free to actively listen, facilitate discussion, call on people as necessary, and remain focused on the task.

It's important that you understand the potential of the tools you have available and have an investment in (after all, you or someone in the organization is paying for them). You don't have to be a master of the technology itself. It matters less who pushes the buttons than that your goals are achieved. It won't happen, though, if the leader doesn't set a good example.

Show up in person

The ultimate rich form of communication is in-person, one-on-one conversation. Just because there are ways to connect electronically doesn't mean that you never again have to drive across town or hop on a plane. Consider questions like these: What are the circumstances when you should meet your team members? How often is it worth investing in that effort and expense? The dividends may well outweigh the direct cost/benefit analysis. Just because your team is remote doesn't mean you can't ever be face-to-face. Fight for the budget and resources to make it happen.

How to Get There

We have framed this chapter in terms of you as a leader and how and when you pick the tools to use. While all of that is true, we are talking about a team here. If you want technology to work most effectively for everyone, everyone needs to be involved in a conversation about it. Top-down edicts that declare "we're going to use this tool" generally encounter resistance. Invite your team to talk about which tools to use under what circumstances. From that conversation, individuals will find what works for them, and the team can come to some common ground rules or expectations about how and when technology is used. You get higher levels of engagement and adoption, and there'll be less whining all the way around. Note that some of the decisions might not be what you would have picked or are most comfortable with, *but that's your job.*

Pause and Reflect

▶ Which tools are you most comfortable with?

▶ Which tools are you least comfortable with?

▶ If you were to use them, how might they help add value to your communication efforts?

▶ Who can you reach out to as a mentor or teacher to help you get better at using these tools?

Online Resources

For more resources go to:

LongDistanceLeaderBook.com/Resources

If you want to have more effective conference calls, request **Conference Call Checklist.**

If you want help deciding which features to use in your webmeeting, request the **Virtual Presentation Checklist.**

Section Four Summary

So What?

- What is one area in which you're engaging others well?
- What is one area in which you can improve the way you engage with others—especially those who are remote from you?

Now What?

- What are specific action steps you can take to engage others more effectively?
- When will you begin?
- What help will you need?
- Where will you start?

Section Five

Understanding Ourselves

How we lead ourselves in life impacts how we lead those around us.

—Michael Hyatt, entrepreneur and former CEO,
Thomas Nelson

Section Five Introduction

We've talked about the focus of leadership—outcomes (where we are going) and others (the people who help us get there). Now we will talk about the core of leadership—ourselves. This is harder to talk about for several reasons.

- As humans we aren't very good at self-awareness.

- We have egos. Some people have overinflated opinions of themselves, and others have less than stellar self-esteem.

- It is just uncomfortable. If you are wondering if this section is even necessary, we'll just say, yes, it is.

Let's dive in.

If you're a believer in servant leadership, you put yourself last, or at least behind other stakeholders. As we have shown, and the Three O Model describes, we believe this is the only way you can lead. Taken to the extreme, focusing on others can lead to sublimating yourself and to not taking care of your mental, physical, and social well-being. If you have vacation days piled up, or your spouse complains you are working while on the beach, you know what we mean.

If you're a "command and control" type leader, the inability to always know what's going on and making sure you agree with it can be frustrating and make you crazy. You try to constantly gather data, which interferes with people getting their work done. It is exhausting to try to keep up with every detail, and no one wants to work for a micromanager. This approach also makes you a whole lot less fun to work with.

Worst of all, if you are striving to be a servant leader and are fearful of exhibiting too much control, you may end up second-guessing yourself, looking inconsistent, unclear, and indecisive.

Regardless of the kind of leader you are or aspire to be, you can't really focus on the desired outcomes or engage with your team without looking at the one constant—yourself. A leader who is physically exhausted, mentally drained, and socially isolated is not going to be effective.

We need to be honest about how we're doing and take care of ourselves. While we are generally not the first people you would associate with Oprah, we do adhere to one of her core precepts: you can't take care of others if you don't take care of yourself first. If you're stressed and drained physically, spiritually, and mentally, and you lack self-awareness of how you are impacting others, you can't be an effective leader no matter where you and your team works.

Just in case you still aren't convinced this section is important to you as a Long-Distance Leader . . .

In our survey of leaders, we found that the vast majority of them say for the most part they do a pretty good job of leading at a distance. Where there are challenges, they fall into three main areas:

- Communicating and making sure the messages are understood

- Knowing the status of work before deadlines loom so stress is lower and odds of success increase

- Coaching and managing performance

These concerns are a major part of the leader's job. As our survey showed, many leaders may be getting the outcomes right, but they are worried about how they are supporting their teams and are quite unclear about how their own performance is perceived.

And besides, who wants to settle for doing "all right, most of the time"?

Chapter 14

Getting Honest Feedback

Rule 14: Seek feedback to best serve outcomes, others, and ourselves.

Feedback is the breakfast of champions.

—Ken Blanchard, management expert and
leadership author

Nicole wants to be an effective leader. She works hard, trying to keep up with the latest leadership practices. But all that effort sometimes leaves her frustrated and confused. She wants to know how she is doing and often second-guesses herself. At the end of the day, she doesn't have a clear picture of how successful she is. This leaves her more than frustrated; it severely hampers her confidence too.

When you work apart from those you lead, you typically lack the instantaneous feedback needed to function at a high level. As leaders, if we don't get regular, honest feedback from our people, it's easy to get excited about the wrong things or ignore inconvenient facts. This can lead to everything from seeming foolish to making decisions that are doomed to fail. How many requests have you made of people that you would have changed or stopped if you could've seen the terrified look on the person's face? In the conference room or on the shop floor you would see that look—but over the phone or in an email, not so much. What mechanisms exist to get the input needed to make good decisions?

Generating Ideas

The leader's job is to dream big *and* sweat the small stuff. Because our brain is always working, we have hundreds of thoughts an hour. Some are valuable ("we should update our branding"), some are musings that may lead nowhere ("what would happen if we opened a Denver office?"), and many are questionable ("handlebar mustaches are cool, right?"). To sort these ideas and decide which to proceed with, you need feedback.

Wayne once worked for someone he respected greatly. He also feared every time she came to the office from out of town, because a lot of her conversations began with, "So, I was reading this article on the plane . . ."

Inevitably, she would have read something that got her thinking on her transcontinental flight. She noodled the idea over and over, playing out different "what if" scenarios in her mind. Being a positive person, she began to see the possibilities and even began to think about implementation, results, and what success would look like. By the time she arrived in the regional office, she was bubbling with enthusiasm for the plan and asking people to start work on it.

The problem was there were always new plans, and while some of them were excellent, even more contradicted previous priorities or initiatives, or had consequences she hadn't considered. Because saying "for the love of all that's holy, stop reading on airplanes!" was a nonstarter, Wayne had to step up and say, "Can we stop and think about this for a moment?" Often the ideas were killed or at least scaled back to something manageable. It helped that she was a reasonable person, open to that kind of feedback.

We aren't suggesting you stop thinking or being enthusiastic about your ideas. You must remember, though, to share and gain feedback on the ideas before you unilaterally decree action that might scare, alienate, or confuse your team.

Listening to the Right Voices

Of course, it's not simply the positive, action-oriented, idea-generating voices in your head that get your attention. You are also at the mercy of negative self-talk and pessimism that can de-motivate or immobilize you. When you can get out of your own head and still listen to the ideas of others, you can get past the negative thinking. If you are alone much of the time, it's not easy to get that interaction.

When your team is remote, it always takes effort to talk with them. Too often, the conversations become transactional and to the point. It is bad enough that leaders don't always ask for feedback—and even more often team members are reluctant to offer it—but this dynamic is made worse at a distance. Additionally, there is a difference between being alone and being lonely. Scientists tell us that being alone with our thoughts is good and helpful; we need time to think, daydream, relax, and refresh. Prolonged isolation, though, can have a serious impact on our behavior, mood, and even health. Even the most introverted among us requires some social interaction. This isolation, as we have mentioned several times in the book, needs to be a real concern for you, and as a concern for you with all your remote team members too. Because of that, you must be vigilant and intentional in asking for feedback not just on your ideas but on how you are doing overall.

Finally, as a reminder: the dark side of being a dedicated, caring leader is that it's easy to diminish your own needs to the point where you're caring so much about everyone else you don't take proper care of yourself.

Data vs. Context

In our survey, many people referenced the problem of getting "good information" to make decisions and plan strategy. It's important to understand that information comes in two forms: data and context.

Data is relatively easy to get. How many units did we sell last month? Do customers like our latest offering? Are we attracting the right people to our organization? These questions can be answered with numbers, and it is likely you and your team can access that information no matter where you work. Technology has made it relatively simple to find that kind of information when you need it.

Context, on the other hand, translates the raw data, turning it into information that's actually useful. For example, if you sold 2,500 widgets this month but normally sell 1,000, that's good news. If 5,000 is a normal month, there's a problem. Still, it's essentially data compared to other data. But how do your people feel about that? Are they motivated and excited, or discouraged and uninspired? The actions you take and the way you communicate can vary greatly depending on their reactions.

Will your speech intended to inspire them light a fire or scorch them, reducing their motivation to ashes? Before sending out that email or calling that town hall meeting, you need to check your assumptions. How we process and respond to both the data and the context will determine both our actions and the actions of those we lead. But where does a leader gain that context? It usually comes through feedback of one sort or another.

Soliciting feedback can help you communicate and lead far more effectively.

As we've said, when you walk the plant floor or stand in the middle of the cubicle farm where people are working, you can sense the mood of the team. When you sit in your home office five hundred miles from the nearest employee, you're drawing conclusions based on how you feel about the situation, what you've seen in a few email threads, or what you heard in one quick conversation with a team member. Soliciting feedback can help you communicate and lead far more effectively.

Soliciting Information and Feedback

The natural reaction when faced with a challenge is to find a small number of people you trust and ask, "What do you think?" That's a good start, yet it may not be enough. Remember the inherent power imbalance. If you hold positional authority over people, their answers will be, to some extent, colored by the fact that you impact their life in many ways, including having the authority to fire them.

The TV show *Undercover Boss* demonstrated this beautifully (if a little painfully for those of us in positions of authority). The CEO of a company would wear a disguise and go out among rank-and-file employees in the business to see how things were really operating and to solicit feedback about his or her performance without the barrier of positional authority. Whether the news was good or bad, the leaders were always surprised by what they learned and were concerned about the gap between their perception of what was happening and the reality of work. While there may be some brand-building advantages for the company by participating in the show, fundamentally, these CEOs go to tremendous effort to get feedback that they can't get otherwise.

This isn't a new concept. *The Arabian Nights* tells of wise sultans who went out in disguise at night to see what was really happening in their cities. The lessons are the same: no matter how benevolent and beloved you are, or think you are, as a leader, getting honest feedback is complicated. Yet how else can you check your assumptions, evaluate decisions more effectively, and lead most effectively in support of both outcomes and others?

When soliciting feedback on yourself, especially as a leader, keep some things in mind:

- *Start with existing evidence.* Before going to individuals, go back through relevant files, email threads, and meeting notes. How are people feeling? What are they thinking about how you're doing and the decisions you're making?

- *Identify people you trust.* Don't confuse this with people you like or who always say yes to your ideas. Trusted advisors can come from many sources: people you know who will tell you the truth as they see it regardless of your position; those who care about you and your success; coworkers with technical expertise that you don't possess; and anyone with firsthand information about the other stakeholders such as employees, customers, or regulators. *Note: If this list of people, especially on your own team, is small, you have a problem! Review the Trust Triangle and get honest with yourself to see why this might be.*

- *Ask open-ended questions.* Remember that no matter how sincere your quest may be, you're still the boss asking, "Do you think this will work?" Since you're asking, the assumption is you think it will, or if you're scowling about it, they know you're skeptical and they probably should be too. A better way to ask is, "Based on what you've heard, what about this would work? What would be a problem? How do you think people will respond, and why?" Make them truly open, and not presumptive.

- *Use the PIN technique when seeking feedback.* PIN stands for "positive, interesting, and negative." By using this technique yourself and encouraging those around you to use it, there's a good chance you'll get more honest answers and be more able to accept what you receive.

  - *Positive.* Describe what is good or valuable about the idea, situation, or behavior. By starting positive, defenses don't immediately go up. This improves the effectiveness of the conversation and the application of the information.

  - *Interesting.* Since the situation or idea might be complex, discuss it a bit further—this is often where trust can be built in the feedback conversation. Discussing what's interesting is a neutral way of identifying things we don't know or assumptions people have.

  - *Negative.* Share the objections, concerns, and negative consequences of the idea, action, or behavior. Once they know the positive aspects have been acknowledged, people are more willing to listen to objections or roadblocks.

  This technique works best over time and needs to be modeled constantly. If you respond to questions this way, over time this will be the way your team communicates.

- *Have these conversations as richly as possible.* You know when communicating with people over the phone, you can't see the gleam in their eyes or if they are rolling them as you speak. If you really want feedback and input, take the time and use the tools in the ways we've discussed. Schedule the conversation, block sufficient time, and use the tools at your disposal. Use your webcams, phone calls, and meeting tools.

- *Have the conversations over time.* If what you're considering is really important, people may do their best thinking before and after the conversation. If you want good insight, people should be able to prepare for the conversation (fly-by requests don't always get you deep thinking, since people were doing something else first). Then the conversation happens in an honest and candid way, but how often have you hung up the phone and realized there was something you hadn't thought of or should have phrased another way? Using asynchronous methods like email (or better, shared folders or documents where people can update at will and they can be referred to easily) will allow for people to add value to their original thoughts. It also gives you the chance to go over them again and reevaluate the feedback.

One of the best ways to build your self-awareness as a leader is by using a 360 Assessment. This is a way to gather anonymous feedback from your team, your peers, and your boss(es) and can include outside stakeholders like customers and suppliers. Many organizations already do this as part of the performance review process. There are a couple of caveats to this:

- It must be truly anonymous.

- The data is only as good as the questions you ask.

For this reason, many leaders and organizations turn to outside parties to conduct these surveys. The Kevin Eikenberry Group offers this service, but so do hundreds of other capable consultants and organizations. We believe the process and coaching that goes with it is more important than the survey itself—not because the questions don't matter, but because there are plenty of good instruments. The process can seem time consuming, but like the sultan and many "undercover bosses" have found, the results can be eye opening.

Pause and Reflect

- ▶ Are you getting enough feedback from others?
- ▶ How confident are you in the quality of that feedback?
- ▶ Do you regularly ask for it?
- ▶ Who will give you honest feedback?
- ▶ How open are you to feedback?

Chapter 15

Your Beliefs and Self-Talk

Rule 15: Examine your beliefs and self-talk—they define how you lead.

Self-esteem is the reputation we acquire with ourselves.
—Nathaniel Branden, author

Nathan had been a successful individual contributor and was promoted to leadership. Although he doubted his skills, he was leading people doing work like he had done, so he felt he was doing fairly well. Senior leaders thought he was doing better than that—they promoted him again. Now he finds himself leading people in three countries doing work he's never done. He lies awake at night wondering if he's really up to the challenge, and he is sure he'll be exposed as unqualified for his job. He wonders if he can ever succeed in this situation.

Good leaders require a relatively healthy self-image. After all, if you don't think you are correct a good percentage of the time, or somewhat capable, or the right woman for the job, you likely wouldn't find yourself in this position. Unless you are a complete sociopath, however, the voices in your head aren't always supportive or positive.

Remember the Walt Disney movie *Pinocchio*? One of the heroic characters in that movie was Jiminy Cricket. While he often sounded like a stick in the mud and a drag, he was there to remind the lad that if he engaged in certain behavior, he'd never become a real boy. Sometimes Pinocchio listened, often he didn't, but at least he wasn't working solely by the unchecked whims of his wooden heart.

In essence, Jiminy was an *auriga*. The auriga was a servant of the Roman emperor, whose job, according to legend, was to stand behind him during large public events and whisper, *memento homo*—"remember, you are just a man"—so that the love of the crowd and the celebration of power wouldn't go to the emperor's head. It didn't make them popular, but the job was valuable.

What if the auriga was a totally negative downer, saying things like, "You're an idiot, nobody likes you," instead of providing a healthy and necessary warning, such as, "Are you sure you want to do that?" How motivated would Caesar be to make the tough decisions or implement any kind of change? Too much of pessimism and "programming" would change how he led and drastically change his results.

What we believe about ourselves dictates how successful we will be. And, our beliefs are formed and reinforced by how we talk to ourselves. Asking questions and checking your assumptions is natural and necessary. Running yourself down and focusing on the negative is terribly destructive. The good news about talking to yourself is that you can change the conversation any time.

Here are some warning signs that your internal dialogue is going in an unhealthy direction, as well as how to steer it onto a more positive path:

- *"You're an idiot. That's the worst idea ever."* Really? Ever? At times like this, it's okay to revert to middle school and ask yourself, "Says who?" If you take that question seriously, it takes you back to the neutral facts. What evidence is there to support or deny your idea or premise? First of all, it's highly unlikely you're an idiot. And it's even more certain it's not the worst idea ever.

- *"I can't do this."* The words we use matter. "Can't" is a statement of fact. It cannot be done—it defies the natural laws of the physical world (e.g., I truly *cannot* lift an elephant with my bare hands). To say I can't hit you with a shovel is literally not true (because I am physically capable of doing so), but it might not be a good idea. When you get frustrated to the point of saying you can't do something, change the word. "I haven't yet figured out how to . . ." or "up until now I haven't been able to do it" are different ideas entirely. Changing the wording recognizes there are difficulties but still accepts the possibility of success, which changes your internal motivation. It also suggests you might need help from elsewhere. Maybe the problem you're trying to solve requires a different solution, but when you are stuck in "I can't," it is hard to see that. You absolutely cannot lift an elephant with your bare hands, but if an elevated pachyderm is what you want, the nearby rope and pulleys might be of assistance. Just because the way you are trying doesn't work doesn't mean the goal is unattainable. It just means you need to stop doing what you're doing and take another look. The same goes for words like "won't," "never," and "impossible."

- *"I'm a fraud and I will be exposed."* This feeling, known as "impostor syndrome," is estimated to affect over 70 percent of leaders.[1] Here are some simple techniques to help address this monster:

  - *Check your assumptions.* Recognize your "I can'ts" for what they are. When in doubt, ask, "Says who?"

  - *Accept positive feedback as valid.* When people tell you how smart or capable you are, believe them and don't dismiss or downplay it. Why would they say it if they didn't see something positive?

  - *Get help.* Remember that even the best and brightest go to others for help, feedback, and answers.

  - *Consider past success.* You've had success in the past, you will have more in the future. Think back to a similar challenge and how you addressed that.

  - *Treat yourself like you would any other competent person.* Don't accept feedback from yourself you wouldn't offer to anyone else. Would you call someone else "totally useless" or worse? Probably not, because it would only make things worse and not address the real problem. Are you different from anyone else?

- *"I've just been lucky so far."* Las Vegas is built on one simple premise: luck only gets you so far, and there's really no such thing. Don't denigrate your past performance or successes.

When you notice you are mired in this negative self-talk, a break may help. Take a walk or indulge in some menial chore that doesn't take too much brainpower. Take time to reflect on your past successes, and ask yourself positive questions. The PIN technique described in the last chapter works for us as well as with others. Why treat other people better than you treat yourself?

Another simple way to address self-talk is to stop talking to yourself and talk to other humans. Schedule a coaching call with an employee. Touch base with former colleagues, who will probably remind you what a rock star you were when you worked together. Call your mom—hearing a voice that's happy to hear yours is an instant pick-me-up.

It takes a conscious effort to reach out to other people, especially when wallowing in negativity, but even the most casual social interaction gets you out of your own head and allows you to replenish your courage and self-worth.

Pause and Reflect

▶ What are your beliefs about yourself as a leader?

▶ How are they helping or hindering your progress and success?

▶ How often does negative self-talk interfere with your confidence or decision making?

▶ When you are caught in a cycle of negative self-talk, what's one thing you can do immediately to refocus your energy in a positive way?

Chapter 16

Setting Reasonable Boundaries

Rule 16: Accept that you can't do it all—you shouldn't try anyway.

---

*Nobody's life is ever all balanced. It's a conscious
decision to choose your priorities every day.*

—Elisabeth Hasselbeck, co-host, *The View*

Allison is a wife and mother of two young boys. She's worked hard to become a project manager and is proud of her accomplishments. She lives in Chicago, and her latest project involves teams in New York, San Francisco, and New Delhi. Because of the geography, communication is a challenge. Talking to any member of the team requires adjusting for time zones and means someone—usually her—is working outside their normal work hours. These demands are tough on her children and spouse, and she *wants* to spend more time with them too. She's feels burned out, exhausted, and knows if she wants to keep her job—and her life—she'll have to find a way to manage it all.

The list of clichés about leadership that we tell ourselves is long. Here are just three:

- "I wouldn't ask my people to do anything I'm not willing to do."

- "The buck stops here."

- "I may not have done it, but I'm responsible for it."

There is truth in each, which is why they are clichés. The problem is that today the work never stops. We hear how business is "24/7/365." The business may never stop, but you are mortal and cannot work that way.

Don't argue—you can't, even if you try.

One of the greatest challenges you face is finding the balance between being responsible to your organization and its people and taking care of yourself so that you can be both highly effective in your leadership role and fully functional as a human being, spouse, partner, neighbor, or productive member of society.

In the 1950s, there was much talk of "the Man in the Gray Flannel Suit," the stereotypical New York businessman who spent all his energy on business, hustling to or from the office but never really relinquishing the role when he got home.[1] This often resulted in the disintegration of his family and, ultimately, his life. But back then all the business took place in one city or time zone and there was no email or cell phones, so the workday eventually ended.

Now, the days seem to blend one into the other. Just when the Boston office is closing down for the night, you can focus on San Francisco, and then there's the rep in Singapore you need to talk to, and who knows what time it is in Bangalore, but if the folks in Boston are going to have what they need you'll have to answer their questions and . . . the cycle repeats itself.

Our survey revealed that many respondents feel terrible about not setting boundaries around their personal time. They fail to set limits on answering phone calls and emails because people rely on them. They also know that they are not giving proper attention to the important parts of their lives, like their family or their hobbies. No matter what they do, they're letting someone down, including themselves.

One of the important challenges about the new virtual remote workplace is how to make yourself accessible to your team while still maintaining personal balance. Working from home allows you to be in physical proximity to your family more often, but does that matter when you're answering email during your kid's soccer match and miss their game-winning goal? It's one thing to tell yourself "just don't answer emails" or "you're off work, so stop working," but it isn't all that helpful. Good leaders have high expectations for themselves that make finding work/life balance hard.

Wayne was working for a company with a big staff of contractors scattered across the country. He was asking them to take on a job and got pushback. "But I wouldn't ask you to do anything I wouldn't do myself" was his exasperated response. One of them stopped and asked, "Yeah, but is there anything you wouldn't do?" The question was valid—what were the limits to his willingness to work? He also realized that he had few, and had done a lot of things that were straining both his health and relationships. True, he wasn't asking people to do anything he wasn't willing to do, but was he willing to do things he'd never ask of anyone else? And should it be done at all?

How can you ensure that you are taking care of your personal time, family responsibilities, and general health while living up to your responsibilities? When you set the bar high for yourself, that becomes the bar for everyone else. Remember, not everyone has to work exactly like you, and your behavior might not be the best to emulate anyway. Remember that your remote team members have less behavior to observe, so all your actions, like it or not, are amplified. What are they seeing and amplifying into their own behavior?

Let's start with those responsibilities and a hard truth: if you are so indispensable to the organization that it cannot function without you for a few hours—or days—you're doing it wrong. Put your ego aside for a moment and ask this simple question: *If I got hit by a bus tomorrow, how would my team function?*

If you are so indispensable to the organization that it cannot function without you for a few hours—or days—you're doing it wrong.

There is a lot of power in that question, because it forces you to look at the things that encroach on your boundaries.

- *Do your people know what they should be doing?* If people are coming to you constantly for decisions or approval, consider the possible reasons. If they don't know what they should be doing, it's likely time for training or coaching. If they do know but come to you anyway, is it because they lack confidence? Or are you second-guessing them, so they decide it is just easier to ask you first? Make sure your people are empowered to make decisions and take action.

- *Are you the only source for answers?* Often people come to their boss for information, but usually that is because they either don't know where else to go or lack faith in those resources. As a leader, are you helping people understand where to find the help they need and encouraging them to get it? Or, when they ask, do you answer from ego or because you want to be helpful? If you are not actively encouraging them to depend on each other, you're making them more reliant on you. If you don't already have an online, asynchronous resource center (shared files, SharePoint, something . . .), maybe it's time add them.

- *Do you have the right people in the right roles?* If you log off for the night and worry that Alice in Dallas can't handle things for an hour or two, what are you going to do about it? Either you have to help Alice get to the point where your trust in her allows you to sleep at night, or get someone in that job who will. If you don't trust the people in place to do their jobs, you'll overcompensate by getting involved yourself—and there goes that trip to the gym.

- *Do you guard your time?* It's one thing to say you'll stay off email at 2:00 a.m. but quite another to do it. If you will be unavailable for three hours to see the kids' Christmas pageant, do people know you are going to be out of touch? They don't need to know why (although it might not be a bad idea, and a good model for your folks), but if you use your status updates, voice mail messages, and other tools to let people know what's going on, it will remove some of the stress for everyone. If they are confident you'll get back to them in a timely manner, they probably won't send an IM, a text, an email, *and* a carrier pigeon after you. Also, if you're answering emails at odd times, for whatever reason, let them know you don't expect the same from them—or that you don't expect immediate responses to yours.

- *Are you answering email and phone calls on vacation?* Many of us try to sneak time to answer emails even when we're on vacation. The problem is that if you're not disconnecting periodically, you may increase your stress or guilt about not being available and not receive the benefits of downtime. If you are going to work while on vacation, you are just working remotely from the beach.

Look at your organization's processes and workflow. Where are you being drawn in unnecessarily? Are there times when you are not critical to the process? If there aren't, could there be? Who else in your organization could take on some of those responsibilities?

We've already talked about delegation in chapter 8, but it is worth mentioning here again. When you delegate successfully, you set your team up to succeed and give yourself the freedom to set healthy personal boundaries too.

Pause and Reflect

- ▶ Do you feel that you have set good (defendable) boundaries between your work and personal time?

- ▶ Specifically, what activities encroach on that time?

- ▶ How might you reduce time spent on that activity?

- ▶ What is one thing you currently do that could be done by someone else?

- ▶ Who is that person?

- ▶ What would it take to give them the responsibility while ensuring success?

- ▶ How will you let the rest of your organization know about this?

- ▶ How will you enforce it?

- ▶ What help do you need?

Chapter 17

Setting Personal Priorities

Rule 17: Balance your priorities to be a Remarkable Long-Distance Leader.

I learned that we can do anything, but we can't do everything . . . at least not at the same time. So think of your priorities not in terms of what activities you do, but when you do them. Timing is everything.

—Dan Millman, author

Donald is an experienced sales manager who has busted his hump to become VP of international sales. He finds the work exhilarating, and he's proud of reaching his career goals. Since his children have grown and moved out of the house, he should have plenty of time to get his work done without distractions. Yet, he doesn't feel as good as he should. Physically, he's worn out and now, at the busiest time of the year, he finds himself listless and not as enthusiastic as he knows he needs to be. His team is complaining that he's working them too hard and isn't really listening to their concerns. He's altered vacation plans twice, and his wife is no happier than his team members. This should be the high point of his career, but it sure doesn't feel like it.

If you are still reading, we are confident that you think of yourself last. As we talked about throughout the book, Outcomes and Others do come before

Ourselves. That doesn't mean we surrender our humanity, our health, or our sanity. There is a difference between self-preservation and selfishness.

There is a difference between self-preservation and selfishness.

Let's start with values. Your values determine how you decide what is truly important to you. Our goal isn't to suggest what your values are but rather to urge *you* to be clear on what they are.

So, what is important to you?

When you ask questions about what is important to you, and answer honestly, you will begin to see that the barriers to managing your time are mostly of your own construction. Everyone has the same amount of time—the question is how will you use it. As Kevin says in *Remarkable Leadership*, time management is really *choice* management. If you aren't clear on your values, you can't make clear choices on how you are using your time.

Knowing your values allows you to prioritize your activities. For example, if you need spiritual balance, working on the finance reports on Sunday might be a bad call. If you need physical exercise to be happy and productive, get to the gym—that time to yourself won't undo all your good work for the week.

We aren't saying making changes to regain control will be easy. First, you need to help people understand how best to work with you. As a simple example, if your email in-box has become unmanageable, encourage people to help you prioritize your messages. When they absolutely need you to read and respond, they should put you on the "To" line. For those things that are merely keeping you in the loop or don't require immediate action, put your name on the "cc" line instead. This will help you spend your time on things that matter, and people won't expect you to respond to everything they send.

Even though this is about you, you'll need help and support to make these changes. Ask people you trust to help you manage your time. Most will be happy to help. If you need an accountability partner, find one. If your goal is to stop answering email in the middle of the night, have someone you trust who will call you on it. Reminding you that that email saying "thanks" went out at 2:00 a.m. will bring you back to your senses.

If you haven't yet, make a list of things that are important to you, and ask yourself: Am I satisfied with the time I'm giving them? If the answer is no, try to identify small blocks of time you can dedicate to them. Typical items on the list are:

- Physical exercise

- Time with my spouse

- The kids' bedtime (or ball game or recital)

- Spiritual practices

- Time with friends

- Reading and self-development

- Time with a hobby

Hobbies and unstructured leisure time are more important than you think. Activities that take your brain away from work will often spark some of your best thinking and make you happier and easier to live with. If Albanian klezmer music is your thing, go to a concert. Join a band. Turn your phone off in the car and crank your tunes until you feel better. It doesn't need to make sense to anyone else. Kevin's obsessed with John Deere tractors. Seriously, it's a thing. He goes to auctions and slows down when he sees anything green in a field. The team teases him about it, but it makes him a happier and more well-rounded person. Whatever floats your boat matters. Take it seriously.

None of this is new information, and we don't want to sound trite. But just because you've heard it before doesn't mean you're comfortable guarding your personal time and energy. If you were, you'd already have greater balance and be less stressed. You have to give yourself the same permission to engage with yourself you'd allow any member of your team. Take it as seriously as you engage with the Organization and Others, and for all the same reasons.

Pause and Reflect

▶ What is your proudest current accomplishment as a leader?

▶ What is one thing in your personal life you are proud of that doesn't involve your work?

▶ What is one thing in your personal life that should be getting more of your time than you're currently allotting?

Section Five Summary

So What?

- How prepared do you feel to aid others in reaching your desired outcomes?

- What is one area where you can improve the way you take care of yourself so you can be most valuable to others?

Now What?

- What specific actions can you take to be a more confident remote leader?

- What are specific action steps you can take to take more care of yourself?

- When will you begin?

- What help will you need?

Section Six

Developing Long-Distance Leaders

Chapter 18

Questions to Ask about Developing Long-Distance Leaders

Rule 18: Ensure your leadership development prepares Long-Distance Leaders.

The growth and development of people
is the highest calling of leadership.

—Harvey Firestone, founder,
Firestone Tire and Rubber Co.

Audrey is in the training department at an international tech company. She's struggling with a paradox. On the one hand, there are requests from individual leaders and managers who want help adjusting to the differences in leading people who aren't in their location. On the other hand, senior management is shrinking training budgets and wondering why the current leadership development efforts aren't more effective. She's wondering if they need to scrap their entire legacy leadership training, or if can they find a way to adjust their current efforts, without reinventing the wheel.

At the beginning of the book we promised assistance for those of you responsible for developing Long-Distance Leaders in your organizations.

Whether you are an individual manager trying to grow the leadership capabilities of your team or you're in charge of learning and development for a huge corporation, we want to share some additional strategies and approaches to create a plan for growing great leaders in the dispersed workplace.

When considering leadership development, we believe there are three pairs of questions to be considered:

- What kind of organization do you want to be? Does your current culture match this vision?

- What behaviors do you expect from your Long-Distance Leaders? What skills gaps must you address?

- What is your plan for developing and supporting your Long-Distance Leaders? How will the organization support the remote team members?

Let's break each of those down in more detail . . .

What Kind of Organization Do You Want to Be? Does Your Current Culture Match This Vision?

Having a clear picture about how a remote workforce fits into the culture you want to create is an important question. As we said at the start of the book, planned or not, you have a remote or dispersed workforce; that ship has sailed. We encourage you to step back and think about how that impacts and informs your organizational culture now and in the future.

Every company has a culture. That is a very soft, consultant-like phrase, we know. Here is how we define culture: "the way we do things here." It doesn't take much insight to realize that when people work apart from each other, the way things are really done can vary greatly from the culture you think (or hope) you have.

You have a culture; it may not have developed intentionally or be the one you want. In a remote and dispersed workplace, if you don't define and assess the culture you want, you may wind up with something completely unintended.

When everyone works in the same location, that culture is much easier to define and maintain. From the way parking is assigned, to the signage on the door, to the colors on the wall and the giant mission statement posted in the break room, everyone sees and hears a consistent message and picks up their cues both intentionally and by osmosis.

Descriptions of the organization such as "we don't depend much on titles here" are obvious when the CEO parks and walks as far in the rain as everyone else. If you work from home and have never seen the soaked CEO, you may not believe that "titles don't matter" and be unduly stressed when you get a request from her. Organizations need to be intentional and consistent in the messages they send or they will find themselves unintentionally building a culture they didn't intend.

In the entire history of business, there have never been so many people working in so many places at once. It's only logical that there will be successes and failures. There is no magic bullet. A recent example proves this point.

In 2017, IBM (a company historically intentional in its culture building) announced it was ending work from home for some of its employees.[1] At first, it sounded like it was calling everyone back to the mother ship, but in reality, it impacted about 2 percent of the workforce. The reason for the change related to team culture.

Certain groups at IBM depend heavily on collaboration—idea sharing and bouncing off and building on each other's ideas. This is particularly true in project and cross-disciplinary teams, yet this was not happening as well as it did when everyone was co-located. While task completion went way up, as we could have told them, there were fewer great new ideas emerging.

Without guidance, people working remotely and left to their own devices tend to get very task-focused and independent. If that is what you are looking for from your people, you might be fine with that—if you have a team of individual customer service reps, or salespeople focused on their quotas, for example. If you want people to collaborate and build strong relationships, it can be done virtually, but as we've seen it needs to be done intentionally—whether at an individual team or an organizational level. IBM assumed it would happen organically—give smart people the mission and the tools and they'll figure it out—but that's not what happened.

You could argue that IBM overreacted, yet similar changes have occurred at Yahoo, Apple, and other companies that implemented remote working without thinking through the consequences or how working remotely would impact the team. These situations aren't an indictment of the potential for tele-work or an indication of a shift away from remote work. Rather, because things weren't working in those cases, it was appropriate to reexamine policies and make a change by pulling people back to the office.

Your cultural aspirations need to be supported by processes. For example, if using the technology available to build strong remote teams is critical to managing your project, is that supported by your performance review? We're regularly amazed by the number of leaders who are assessed on their "commu-nication skills" but aren't held accountable for their ability to use the tools at their disposal. If contributing to team brainstorms and discussions is a core competency for team members, are they coached on their lack of contribution to virtual meetings or conference calls? Or are people simply allowed to log on, answer email, and claim they were there?

Management expert Peter Drucker has frequently been quoted as saying, "Put good people in a bad system, and the system wins every time." Intention-ally developing a culture means not only educating and empowering leaders but having the whole organization work in concert to achieve those desired behaviors. Some of the most obvious examples are:

- *Human Resources*. Do your organization's performance management sys-tems reflect the reality of how people work today? Do your support sys-tems like the learning management system and annual performance reviews reflect the additional skills and changed dynamics of leading peo-ple and working together from a distance? Are the processes for assessing, rewarding, and promoting teleworkers equal to those of people in the office? If the company expects people to have webmeetings, are they also willing to invest in webcams and headsets so that those meetings can be as effective as possible?

- *Information Technology*. Do your IT people make all the technology deci-sions and provide the training? If so, you may have created unintended cultural problems. For example, if they're concerned about intranet band-width, they may decree that nobody can use webcams. Do you want that decision made in a vacuum, or do you want a real conversation that considers the culture you want and real-world expectations of your leaders before that decision is made?

Too many organizations we consult with have placed limits on what their people can and can't do based on either old thinking or faulty assumptions about what their jobs really entail. One client's IT department chose a virtual training platform they felt would do the job. Unfortunately, that platform didn't work outside the firewall, so teleworkers and people who worked in another country couldn't access it. Had there been more consultation and contributions from end users, problems like this could have been avoided.

What Are Your Expectations of Your Long-Distance Leaders? What Are Their Skill Gaps?

We recommend using your existing competencies as your starting point, then using all three gears in the Remote Leadership Model to frame the discussion about additions or changes driven by leading remotely. Here is some help for those conversations.

Leadership and management

Compare your leadership competency list with the ideas we have talked about in the book. Ask yourself:

- Does your existing competency model accurately reflect the expectations you have of your remote leaders?

- If not, what isn't addressed?

- Do you need to be more explicit or specific on any of the competencies for Long-Distance Leaders?

Leading remotely means there are certain skills and knowledge that may need to be added to, or at least addressed, in your current learning offerings. Before you say, "Yes, we have coaching and communication workshops," think about the nuances that will lead to success in this new environment in areas like coaching, delegation, communication, leading meetings, building relationships, setting goals, and more. Leaders need to be aware of both the dynamics of working remotely and specific techniques to help address and mitigate those differences.

If these learning opportunities aren't already available to your leaders, they should be, and in a variety of methodologies. This includes traditional classroom, virtual training and e-learning, self-paced instruction, and perhaps blended approaches.

Tools and technology

This gear most directly impacts how leaders make the shift from traditional leadership to leading in a remote or virtual environment. Consider these questions to clarify your organizational expectations of your Long-Distance Leaders.

- Which tools do you want them to use, and when should they be used? This is the richness vs. scope discussion. Do people know how to use Skype/WebEx/SharePoint/whatever? And by "use," we mean more than knowing how to fire up the application. Provide the expectations and guidance based on our recommendations in this book.

- What does "use the tools effectively" look like? This includes both the mechanics of the tools (do they know which button to push?) but also helping them leverage Skype/WebEx/whatever to facilitate an engaging, interactive, and effective meeting, which is more about facilitation and leadership than technology.

Skills and impact

Having tools are only helpful when you can use them properly and effectively.

- Do your leaders use the tools in an impactful way? Understanding what leaders need to do, and the tools at their disposal, is important, but they also need to use those tools well. If leaders don't feel confident using technology, they won't be nearly as effective as they should be.

- Do people have the chance to practice? People need to practice and receive coaching and feedback when the pressure isn't on. You won't solve this confidence gap with the online tutorials that came with your software license. This is a major reason why organizations don't get maximum return on their technology investment.

What Is Your Plan for Developing and Supporting Your Long-Distance Leaders? How Will the Organization Support the Remote Team Members?

With answers to all the questions above, you are now prepared to create a plan to develop your Long-Distance Leaders. Too often there isn't a real plan; rather a decision is made to "add a course" or "send some people" to a workshop without context and a clear purpose for those attending or the organization as a whole.

Notice we didn't include the word "training" in the question. That was intentional. We believe the focus of "developing and supporting" should be learning and not simply training. When you change your perspective to learning, you will do three things:

- *Connect learning to the work.* We are sometimes asked to travel to organizations and teach people how to lead teams remotely. While we can do that, doesn't it make more sense to teach people how to effectively communicate using technology by using the technology so they can see it used well? Otherwise it is like teaching people to swim in a gym. Learning happens fastest and best when it is directly related to the work people do, in the way they do it. It also needs to be realistic; helping people learn to communicate effectively in a remote environment doesn't help if intranet bandwidth and company policy make webcams impossible, or VPN connections to the company's servers are unreliable. Encouraging people during a workshop to collaborate and work together is a lost cause if all their key performance indicators (KPIs) are individually focused.

- *Make learning available in different ways.* If your workplace is a complex mixture of people working in all sorts of locations, in different zones, and on different schedules, shouldn't the ways to learn the related skills reflect this reality? Make sure you have a mix of both asynchronous and synchronous options available to your remote leaders and their teams.

- *Make it a process.* We believe that training is an event, but learning is a process. If you want people to transfer what they are learning to the workplace, change a habit, and build confidence in doing new things, an event alone will always fall short. No one learned to play a piano well by attending a piano skills workshop. We learn skills over time, not all at one time. Coaching (one-on-one or group) and mentoring can and should be included in your leadership development plans.

We are admittedly biased, but we believe that while you don't want to outsource everything we have just described, you also don't likely want to do it all internally either. The nuances in skills and the context of working with people remotely are different than what your training department is likely used to delivering.

Since 2009, Wayne has asked hundreds of trainers who did both online and classroom facilitation if they received any training before being asked to present online training and presentations. For over half of the trainers, the answer was a resounding no—they were expected to figure it out on their own. Fortunately this is changing quickly. While it's not quite the blind leading the blind, it's unfair and ineffective to ask people who are unfamiliar with teleworking or technology to design and deliver learning on these topics.

Finally, although IT is typically tasked with teaching the technology, there are problems with this approach:

- *It takes more than a demonstration.* To truly teach a technology effectively requires context, demonstration, application, and ongoing coaching. Simply recording someone who is proficient in the technology (but not in facilitating learning) and making the recording available is not training. Do your IT people have the resources and expertise to help people really learn these skills?

- *IT is focused on the tool, not the context.* They may not understand how leaders need to use the tool in their work. Someone who uses WebEx for tech support by sharing a screen is going to use it very differently than those who are leading and communicating using the tools. Any training on a tool must be done in the context of how people will use it in real life.

- *Do they know?* Just because they're techies doesn't mean they use the tool properly. We frequently see IT people who have used Skype for Business for a long time but aren't even aware of some of the richer tools associated with it, like surveys and whiteboards. We aren't throwing anyone under the bus—they may never have needed to use those options. It just points out that they might not be the most qualified people to teach your leaders.

The Remote Team

This book is about leadership, and yet we can't talk about developing successful Long-Distance Leaders without acknowledging those on the team who work remotely and need support and additional skills. Teams only function at a high level when everyone has the same understanding of how to make things work in the real world. For example, sharing the Trust Triangle only with leaders but not their team is a mistake.

Consider these questions:

- Do your remote workers understand the organization's mission and vision, goals and strategies, and how their work is aligned? (Remember, many of the cues and reminders available when working on site are lost when working away from the office or plant.)

- Do your individual team members know what is expected of them specifically related to working remotely?

- Do they have the technical skills they need to get their work done?

- Do they have the skills to communicate, build relationships, and generate trust successfully at a distance?

- Do they have options for learning the skills they are missing?

And perhaps most important, how confident are you in your answers to all the questions in this chapter? If you are still reading, you are thinking about helping your Long-Distance Leaders succeed. Ultimately, they can't succeed without a successful team. Make sure you are supporting and developing them too.

Pause and Reflect

We concluded the previous chapters by having you "pause and reflect" on yourself or your team. In this section, our focus is different—we are asking you to think at an organization level. This may involve conversations with people in other departments. We encourage that conversation and the actions they generate.

▶ What is the organizational culture you aspire to?

▶ How does the remote nature of some team members impact that cultural vision?

▶ What behaviors should change to create that culture, especially for the remote team members?

▶ What behaviors and skills do you want your Long-Distance Leaders to exhibit?

▶ What gaps in skills and knowledge exist for your Long-Distance Leaders?

▶ What learning resources and materials do you have that correctly reflect the needs of the Long-Distance Leader?

▶ Which groups or parts of the organization should have a role in the creation of your leadership development plan (besides the training department)?

▶ How can you ensure these stakeholders are aligned so that the leadership development plans meet real-world needs?

Online Resources

For more resources go to:

LongDistanceLeaderBook.com/Resources

To identify the biggest skill and knowledge gaps in your organization directly related to working remotely, request the **Organizational Technology Assessment.**

If you would like more help and ideas, go to RemoteLeadershipInstitute.com or see pages 210–211 for a complete list of our services, thought leadership, and free resources.

Epilogue

Before We Go

Rule 19: When all else fails, remember Rule 1.

Without continual growth and progress, such words as improvement, achievement, and success have no meaning.

—Benjamin Franklin

This book is nearly complete, but we hope your work has just begun.

A book by itself is of little importance. We don't say that out of false modesty; only to put it into the proper context. If we have done our job, this book has done two, maybe three things:

- *It has educated you.* After all, you haven't been reading one of Wayne's novels (yes, he's written some—Google it). You picked up this book to learn something new about leading a team at a distance, to see something in a new way, or perhaps even to confirm that something you have been doing is "right," appropriate, and perhaps even a best practice.

- *It has inspired you.* Education without any inspiration is a dry exercise. With no disrespect to any of your past teachers, you probably took some classes in school that may have educated you but didn't leave you very inspired. We hope you now have more hope, more confidence, and a sense

189

of the value and importance of the acts of leadership, especially when distance makes it even more complex.

- *It has entertained you.* While not as important (perhaps) as the first two things, we could argue that without this, the other two wouldn't have happened. After all, how many books have you read that talk about the building of the pyramids, a football player in the 1960s, and Albanian klezmer music? Our work at Remote Leadership Institute and the Kevin Eikenberry Group is partly based on the notion that learning can and should be fun.

But really, we have aspired to a fourth thing, the real purpose of this book.

- *It has led you to action.* Education, inspiration, and even entertainment are worthy goals, but they are only process goals. The *results* goal here is Application; that you go out and do something. If you aren't more intentional about how you give feedback, if you don't learn to use your technology more effectively, if you don't help people reach the goals that are set, what was the point?

One of the best compliments Kevin received for his book *Remarkable Leadership* was "you can tell this book was written by a trainer. He is continually encouraging you to try what you are learning." Both of us are proud to wear the hat of trainer, teacher, and facilitator of learning. Both of us have spent many hours in a classroom (and on one side of a webcam) helping people from around the world learn new skills and approaches to leading and communicating more effectively. We wrote this book so you could do your work with more skill, effectiveness, and confidence.

But it is just a book.

Now the real (important) work begins.

If you are leaving with tools and the confidence to go try them, we are pleased, proud, and honored.

And while the book may be ending, our commitment to helping those leading at a distance isn't.

At the close of many chapters we have provided links to online resources. These assessments, checklists, and other tools were designed to give you more than the physical book allowed. They are available solely to those who have read the book. Please use them—that is why we created them.

Go to RemoteLeadershipInstitute.com—there you'll find new ideas, new tools, our latest thinking, and much more. We are committed to helping leaders at a distance lead more effectively.

And while you are there, you can find links and phone numbers to contact us. Like all authors, we would love to hear from you, understand the questions we didn't answer (and hopefully give you some insight), hear how what we've written has made a difference, and in general continue the conversation about being more effective as a Long-Distance Leader.

With all the best to you, and with all due respect, now get back to work leading at a distance more effectively.

Notes

Chapter 1

1. The survey was conducted between June and September of 2017 and continues today. To take part in the survey and add your voice, go to http://longdistance leaderbook.com/survey.

2. Jean M. Twenge, *iGen: Why Today's Super-Connected Kids Are Growing Up Less Rebellious, More Tolerant, Less Happy—and Completely Unprepared for Adulthood* (New York: Atria Books, 2017).

Chapter 2

1. Andrew Filev, "The Future of Remote Teams: How to Fine-Tune Virtual Collaboration" (paper presented at PMI® Global Congress 2012—North America, Vancouver, British Columbia, Canada), https://www.pmi.org/learning/library /remote-teams-tune-virtual-collaboration-6022.

2. Bureau of Labor Statistics, "American Time Use Survey—2016 Results," news release no. USDL-17-0880, June 27, 2017, https://www.bls.gov/news.release /pdf/atus.pdf. See also Alina Tugend, "It's Unclearly Defined, but Telecommuting Is Fast on the Rise," *New York Times*, March 7, 2014, https://www.nytimes.com /2014/03/08/your-money/when-working-in-your-pajamas-is-more-productive .html?_r=0.

Chapter 3

1. Karen Sobel Lojeski, *Leading the Virtual Workforce: How Great Leaders Transform Organizations in the 21st Century* (Hoboken, NJ: John Wiley & Sons, 2009).

Chapter 4

1. Based on *The CHAOS Report* (1994) by the Standish Group and revisited in 2007. Although there is considerable debate about the numbers, Jim Highsmith, in *Agile Project Management: Creating Innovative Products*, and other experts have

concluded: "The Standish data are NOT a good indicator of poor software development performance. However, they ARE an indicator of systemic failure of our planning and measurement processes." He goes on to say that you can't use the Standish numbers to show return on investment, but they accurately predict end-user adoption and other cultural barriers to success.

2. Gerald C. Kane, Doug Palmer, Anh Nguyen Phillips, David Kiron, and Natasha Buckley, "Strategy, Not Technology Drives Digital Transformation," *MIT Sloan Management Review* (July 14, 2015), https://sloanreview.mit.edu/projects /strategy-drives-digital-transformation/, and Michael Fitzgerald, Nina Kruschwitz, Didier Bonnet, and Michael Welch, "Embracing Digital Technology: A New Strategic Imperative," *MIT Sloan Management Review* (October 7, 2013), https://sloanreview.mit.edu/projects/embracing-digital-technology/.

Chapter 5

1. For more on servant leadership, see the Robert K. Greenleaf Center for Servant Leadership, https://www.greenleaf.org/what-is-servant-leadership.

2. "Mission Statement of McDonald's," Strategic Management Insight, September 14, 2013, https://www.strategicmanagementinsight.com/mission-statements/ mcdonalds-mission-statement.html.

3. "Google Business Profile and Mission Statement," The Balance, July 13, 2017, https://www.thebalance.com/google-business-profile-2892814.

4. Nicholas Bloom, "To Raise Productivity, Let More Employees Work from Home," *Harvard Business Review*, January-February 2014, https://hbr.org /2014/01/to-raise-productivity-let-more-employees-work-from-home.

5. Justin Kruger and David Dunning, "Unskilled and Unaware of It: How Difficulties in Recognizing One's Own Incompetence Lead to Inflated Self-Assessments," *Journal of Personality and Social Psychology* 77, no. 6 (1999): 1121–1134.

Section 3 Introduction

1. Bloom, "To Raise Productivity," *Harvard Business Review*.

Chapter 7

1. Here is one source for the anecdote, although note Jerry Seinfeld's response to it in the footnote: James Clear, "How to Stop Procrastinating," *James Clear* blog, https://jamesclear.com/stop-procrastinating-seinfeld-strategy.

2. Tomas Laurinavicius, "34 Best Habit Forming Apps of 2017," *tomas laurinavicius* blog, March 30, 2017, https://tomaslau.com/habit-forming-apps.

Chapter 8

1. Victor Lipman, "65% of Employees Want More Feedback (So Why Don't They Get It?)," *Forbes*, August 8, 2016, https://www.forbes.com/sites/victorlipman /2016/08/08/65-of-employees-want-more-feedback-so-why-dont-they-get-it /#43311996914a.

2. Marshall Goldsmith, Laurence S. Lyons, and Sarah McArthur, *Coaching for Leadership: Writings on Leadership from the World's Greatest Coaches*, 3rd ed. (San Francisco: Pfeiffer, 2012).

3. Andrew S. Grove, *High Output Management* (New York: Random House, 1983, 1995).

4. Thomas J. Peters, Robert H. Waterman, *In Search of Excellence: Lessons From America's Best-Run Companies* (New York: HarperCollins, 1982, 2004).

Chapter 11

1. James M. Kouzes, Barry Z. Posner, *The Leadership Challenge: How to Make Extraordinary Things Happen in Organizations*, 6th ed. (Hoboken, NJ: John Wiley & Sons, 2017).

2. Alice F. Stuhlmacher, Maryalice Citera, and Toni Willis, "Gender Differences in Virtual Negotiation: Theory and Research," ResearchGate, July 3, 2007, https:// www.researchgate.net/publication/225629879_Gender_Differences_in_Virtual _Negotiation_Theory_and_Research.

Chapter 12

1. Bettina S. T. Büchel, *Using Communication Technology* (New York: Palgrave, 2001).

Chapter 13

1. Gerald C. Kane, Doug Palmer, Anh Nguyen Phillips, David Kiron, and Natasha Buckley, "Strategy, Not Technology Drives Digital Transformation," *MIT Sloan Management Review* (July 14, 2015), https://sloanreview.mit.edu/projects /strategy-drives-digital-transformation/, and Michael Fitzgerald, Nina Kruschwitz, Didier Bonnet, and Michael Welch, "Embracing Digital Technology: A New Strategic Imperative," *MIT Sloan Management Review* (October 7, 2013), https://sloanreview.mit.edu/projects/embracing-digital-technology

2. Kane, et al., "Strategy, Not Technology," and Fitzgerald, et al., "Embracing Digital Technology," *MIT Sloan*.

3. "True Wireless Confessions: How People Really Use Their Phones," Verizon, April 2015, https://cbsdetroit.files.wordpress.com/2015/06/true-wireless -confessions-june-2015.pdf.

Chapter 15

1. Pauline Rose Clance and Suzanne Imes, "The Imposter Phenomenon in High Achieving Women: Dynamics and Therapeutic Intervention," *Psychotherapy Theory, Research and Practice* 15, no. 3 (1978), http://www.paulineroseclance.com /pdf/ip_high_achieving_women.pdf.

Chapter 16

1. While the term has become commonplace, it refers to the title character of the 1955 novel *The Man in the Gray Flannel Suit* by Sloan Wilson. Gregory Peck starred in the 1956 movie of the same name.

Chapter 18

1. John Simons, "IBM, a Pioneer of Remote Work, Calls Workers Back to the Office," *Wall Street Journal*, May 18, 2017, https://www.wsj.com/articles/ ibm-a-pioneer-of-remote-work-calls-workers-back-to-the-office-1495108802.

Suggested Reading

Bell, Chip R., and Marshall Goldsmith. *Managers As Mentors: Building Partnerships for Learning*. Oakland, CA: Berrett-Koehler Publishers, 2013.

Booher, Dianna. *Communicate Like a Leader: Connecting Strategically to Coach, Inspire, and Get Things Done*. Oakland, CA: Berrett-Koehler Publishers, 2017.

Büchel, Bettina S. *Using Communication Technology: Creating Knowledge Organizations*. New York: Palgrave MacMillan, 2001.

Covey, Stephen M. R. *The Speed of Trust: The One Thing That Changes Everything*. New York: Free Press, 2008.

Drucker, Peter F. *The Effective Executive: The Definitive Guide to Getting the Right Things Done*. New York: HarperCollins, 2006.

Eikenberry, Kevin. *Remarkable Leadership: Unleashing Your Leadership Potential One Skill at a Time*. San Francisco: Jossey-Bass, 2007.

Eikenberry, Kevin, and Guy Harris. *From Bud to Boss: Secrets to a Successful Transition to Remarkable Leadership*. San Francisco: Jossey-Bass, 2011.

Gentry, William. *Be the Boss Everyone Wants to Work For: A Guide for New Leaders*. Oakland, CA: Berrett-Koehler Publishers, 2016.

Kahnweiler, Jennifer B. *The Genius of Opposites: How Introverts and Extroverts Achieve Extraordinary Results Together*. Oakland, CA: Berrett-Koehler Publishers, 2015.

Kouzes, James M., and Barry Z. Posner. *The Leadership Challenge: How to Make Extraordinary Things Happen in Organizations*, 6th ed. Hoboken, NJ: John Wiley & Sons, 2017.

Maxwell, John C. *The 21 Irrefutable Laws of Leadership: Follow Them and People Will Follow You*. Nashville, TN: Thomas Nelson, 2007.

Rad, Parvis F., and Ginger Levin. *Achieving Project Management Success Using Virtual Teams*. Boca Raton, FL: J. Ross Publishing, 2003.

Sayers, Gale, and Al Silverman. *I Am Third: The Inspiration for "Brian's Song,"* 3rd ed. New York: Penguin Books, 2001.

Stanier, Michael Bungay. *The Coaching Habit: Say Less, Ask More, and Change the Way You Lead Forever.* Toronto, ON: Box of Crayons Press, 2016.

Turmel, Wayne. *Meet Like You Mean It: A Leader's Guide to Painless and Productive Virtual Meetings.* Lisle, IL: Achis Marketing Services, 2014.

Zofi, Yael. *A Manager's Guide to Virtual Teams.* New York: AMACOM, 2012.

Acknowledgments

A book like this requires the help of a lot of people and, fittingly, they are scattered far and wide.

First, there's the team we work with every day at the Kevin Eikenberry Group and the Remote Leadership Institute. From Richmond to Phoenix, Chicago to Indianapolis, you continue to amaze us with your hard work, keen insight, and cheerful support. In particular, thanks to Erica Brown for her assistance with the graphics and helping us put our words into pictures.

We're grateful to the team at Berrett-Koehler for their faith in us, as well as their early support for and keeping us focused on this project and keeping us focused on a constantly changing target. Specifically, Neal Maillet and Jeevan Sivasubramaniam, as well as the production team and everyone involved in marketing and promotion, deserve a nod. Without them, you likely wouldn't be reading this. Roger Peterson helped us polish our ideas and create a better book. The guys with the dirty job of cleaning up our copy, Jon Ford and Jonathan Peck, have also done yeoman service.

Finally, to our valued customers: it's our pleasure to serve, work with, and learn from you. It's our sincere hope that this book makes your journey a little less arduous.

Beyond this, here are some personal thoughts from each of us.

From Kevin...
Beyond our overall acknowledgment of the team, I must say more. I believe this book is better because I have the chance to lead this remote team each day. Many of the ideas have been tested and honed through my

interactions with our team. What I have learned from them can't be overstated. Finally, I thank my wife, Lori, for her patience, understanding, and support—not just while writing this book but throughout our lives. She makes me better in every way.

From Wayne . . .

People have been writing leadership books since the Code of Hammurabi, and we merely stand on their shoulders. It would be both rude to ignore and impossible to count them all, but this hopefully adds to the collective wisdom. Also, I must acknowledge my wife, Joan (the Duchess), for all of her unstinting support and incredible patience.

Index

Note: Page numbers followed by *f* indicate a figure on the corresponding page.

About the Authors

Kevin Eikenberry

Kevin Eikenberry is a recognized world expert on leadership development and learning and is the Chief Potential Officer of the Kevin Eikenberry Group. He is creator of the Remarkable Leadership Learning System and the co-founder of the Remote Leadership Institute.

Kevin has spent more than twenty-five years helping organizations across North America and leaders from around the world on leadership, learning, teams and teamwork, communication, and more. His client list includes Fortune 500 companies, small firms, universities, government agencies, and hospitals. Past clients include names you'll recognize: the American Red Cross, Chevron Phillips Chemical Company, Cirque du Soleil, John Deere, Purdue University, Southwest Airlines, and many more.

He is the author of the bestselling books *Remarkable Leadership* and *Vantagepoints on Learning and Life*. He coauthored with Guy Harris another bestseller, *From Bud to Boss: Secrets of the Successful Transition to Remarkable Leadership*, and a companion book titled *My Journey from Bud to Boss*. Beyond these, he is a contributing author to more than fifteen other books.

Kevin's blog is consistently ranked among the world's best and most read leadership blogs. He has been named by Inc.com as one of the top one hundred leadership and management thinkers in the world and is listed as a top leadership speaker and thinker in several other publications.

Wayne Turmel

Wayne Turmel is a co-founder of the Remote Leadership Institute. He has spent the last twenty years or more obsessed by how people communicate at work. His work has helped organizations on four continents develop the communication skills needed to lead people, projects, and teams and to make the adjustment to remote working and virtual teams.

Wayne is the author of several books, including *ASTD's 10 Steps to Successful Virtual Presentations* and *Meet Like You Mean It: A Leader's Guide to Painless and Productive Virtual Meetings*. He's also contributed to almost a dozen other books, and his groundbreaking podcast, *The Cranky Middle Manager Show*, was one of the first leadership podcasts to be included in the list of 50 Top Influential HR Blogs by BNET. His clients have included the American Red Cross, Schneider Electric, Dell, and several departments of the US and Canadian governments.

Marshall Goldsmith has called Wayne "one of the truly unique voices in leadership."

About Our Services

Helping Remote Leaders and Their Teams Succeed

We're confident you found this book helpful, but we also know that it was just the tip of the iceberg. There's more to learn, and the Remote Leadership Institute is here to help. Our website gives you . . .

More tools. Our regularly updated blog shares lessons from clients and our latest thinking on the continually evolving picture of the remote working world. While there are resources you can purchase, most are completely free and ready for you to read, watch, and apply.

More learning opportunities. We offer a variety of learning opportunities, from the complete Remote Leadership Certificate Series, to live, virtually delivered learning events, to on-demand offerings and e-learning tools to place on your LMS.

More help. If you want to talk about the broader organizational needs related to remote leadership and remote work, please reach out to us. You can find all this and more at RemoteLeadershipInstitute.com/LDL, and use promo code BOOK to receive a 25 percent discount on any of our learning products.

For all the tools available as a reader of this book, go to LongDistance-LeaderBook.com/resources.

REMOTE LEADERSHIP

INSTITUTE

More Than Leading at a Distance

You and your leaders are leading, and not just remotely!

This book has helped you think about the challenges and opportunities of leading at a distance, but you likely have other challenges, needs, and questions too.

The Kevin Eikenberry Group exists to help leaders become more effective, confident, and successful since 1993. How can we help you?

Helping senior leaders. Need an outside perspective to reach your business goals and objectives? We help senior leaders succeed through consultation on building a leadership pipeline, leading culture change, and executive coaching.

Helping new and frontline leaders. Do you need support for your new or first-line leaders? Through our Bud to Boss resources, we offer nearly every organizational and individual option to help your new and frontline leaders succeed. We know their challenges, opportunities, and pain, and we help hundreds of these leaders grow each year.

Helping all leaders. Are you looking to build your skills and confidence as a leader, whether you are new or have been doing this for a long time? We help all leaders with a wide variety of learning opportunities and coaching options.

Inspiring and informing teams and individuals. Are you looking for tools and options to engage and grow everyone in your organization? We offer free tools, videos, podcasts, and much more to help all employees engage and grow as a part of your organization.

Learn more at KevinEikenberry.com/LDL.

Sign up for our unique video series at 13 Days to Remarkable Leadership at KevinEikenberry.com/13days to continue your journey and discover how we can help you become the leader you were born to be.

Berrett–Koehler
Publishers

Berrett-Koehler is an independent publisher dedicated to an ambitious mission: Connecting people and ideas to create a world that works for all.

We believe that the solutions to the world's problems will come from all of us, working at all levels: in our organizations, in our society, and in our own lives. Our BK Business books help people make their organizations more humane, democratic, diverse, and effective (we don't think there's any contradiction there). Our BK Currents books offer pathways to creating a more just, equitable, and sustainable society. Our BK Life books help people create positive change in their lives and align their personal practices with their aspirations for a better world.

All of our books are designed to bring people seeking positive change together around the ideas that empower them to see and shape the world in a new way.

And we strive to practice what we preach. At the core of our approach is Stewardship, a deep sense of responsibility to administer the company for the benefit of all of our stakeholder groups including authors, customers, employees, investors, service providers, and the communities and environment around us. Everything we do is built around this and our other key values of quality, partnership, inclusion, and sustainability.

This is why we are both a B-Corporation and a California Benefit Corporation—a certification and a for-profit legal status that require us to adhere to the highest standards for corporate, social, and environmental performance.

We are grateful to our readers, authors, and other friends of the company who consider themselves to be part of the BK Community. We hope that you, too, will join us in our mission.

A BK Business Book

We hope you enjoy this BK Business book. BK Business books pioneer new leadership and management practices and socially responsible approaches to business. They are designed to provide you with groundbreaking and practical tools to transform your work and organizations while upholding the triple bottom line of people, planet, and profits. High-five!

To find out more, visit **www.bkconnection.com.**

Berrett–Koehler
Publishers

Connecting people and ideas
to create a world that works for all

Dear Reader,

Thank you for picking up this book and joining our worldwide community of Berrett-Koehler readers. We share ideas that bring positive change into people's lives, organizations, and society.

To welcome you, we'd like to offer you a free e-book. You can pick from among twelve of our bestselling books by entering the promotional code **BKP92E** here: http://www.bkconnection.com/welcome.

When you claim your free e-book, we'll also send you a copy of our e-newsletter, the *BK Communiqué*. Although you're free to unsubscribe, there are many benefits to sticking around. In every issue of our newsletter you'll find

- A free e-book
- Tips from famous authors
- Discounts on spotlight titles
- Hilarious insider publishing news
- A chance to win a prize for answering a riddle

Best of all, our readers tell us, "Your newsletter is the only one I actually read." So claim your gift today, and please stay in touch!

Sincerely,

Charlotte Ashlock
Steward of the BK Website

Questions? Comments? Contact me at bkcommunity@bkpub.com.

Certified

Corporation
bcorporation.net